MW01520450

TRAPPED
in a
PAINTING

Listen to the universe,
she has all the answers

EMILY P. ZALOTT

 FriesenPress

Suite 300 - 990 Fort St
Victoria, BC, V8V 3K2
Canada

www.friesenpress.com

Copyright © 2020 by Emily P. Zalott
First Edition — 2020

Edited by Barb Davis & Laura Brustenga

All rights reserved.

No part of this publication may be reproduced in any form, or by any means, electronic or mechanical, including photocopying, recording, or any information browsing, storage, or retrieval system, without permission in writing from FriesenPress.

ISBN
978-1-5255-6307-2 (Hardcover)
978-1-5255-6308-9 (Paperback)
978-1-5255-6309-6 (eBook)

1. BIOGRAPHY & AUTOBIOGRAPHY, PERSONAL MEMOIRS

Distributed to the trade by The Ingram Book Company

This book is dedicated to all my wonderful female souls I have had the privilege to travel through this life with. The three women who mean the most too me are my daughters. They keep me going, they give me a purpose and surprise me everyday with their ability to adapt.

My youngest angel is struggling with Lyme Disease. Please keep her and others you know, fighting for their life, in your thoughts and prayers.

"Don't try to swim up stream, just go with the flow".

Emily. P. Zalott

These are my memories, as I recollect them, a Rolodex of verbal diarrhea I found myself spewing out onto paper one day. I've changed the names and places of the real-life members of the family portrayed in this book. I thank them for being part of my family and accepting me as one of their own. I recognize that their memories of the events described in this book may be different than my own. This book was written as therapy to myself.

The book was not intended to hurt the family. Both my publisher and I regret any unintentional harm resulting from the publishing and marketing of *Trapped in a Painting*.

Emily. P. Zallot

This is one woman's story—my story—of how I went from being emotionally beaten by myself and my husband to having a much needed happily ever after. I lost myself, my beliefs. Who was I? Did I like this person I had become?

I believe we become what that other person in the relationship wants us to be unless we are willing to expose the real you. It's about how I was ready to sacrifice it all for my sanity. There was a soul inside my body screaming to escape the solitude, the empty, loveless relationship, but how?

I used my sense of humor, that piece of my true self, to get me through it and discovered that it takes as much energy to laugh as it does to cry. Why not laugh at what life throws you? Ask yourself this? Can you blame life for your mishaps, or is it all you? Isn't life just a big board-game anyway? Are we not the pieces manipulated by our thoughts and actions?

I want to look back at my past, and to do so without regret and instead see the valuable lessons that brought me to her current strength and wisdom. I want to embrace the fullness of my experiences. If you are living without learning, then you will repeat those mistakes over and over again. Once you realize the pattern, you have the power inside you to turn and chose another path. There is a way of new beginnings, of a divine, more powerful future than awaits you.

And if that isn't working for you, and life throws you lemons, don't make lemonade. I say—you need something much stronger.

INTRODUCTION

Window to My Soul

Our emotions color our lives, and mine has been a rainbow. I have always had an eye for art, or was it the eyes of the picture? Ever since I was a little girl. I found myself in my room, sketching for hours. I love the way artists can put their visions on canvas. The French Renaissance period took me to Paris. It was my third visit to the Louvre. I admire the way artists can use their oils, watercolors, and charcoals to bring life to their canvas. They can paint a picture or tell a story, allowing the observer to create their world. When I looked at a painting, I marveled at the way the subject's eyes can follow you and how the artist can make their subject come alive. Eyes are the window to the soul.

My sister and I finally made it through the maze of tourists to the "Mona Lisa." She was much smaller than we expected. They displayed her on a massive wall in a grand room to give viewers a look at her from all angles. It didn't matter where you were in that room; she was looking at you. She was looking at me. What was she saying to me? "Emily gets out of this room, are you not claustrophobic?.

Leonardo DaVinci painted his friend's wife. He was not just a painter but a poet and philosopher. There was more going on with this model. What was going through her head as she sat as a model? Was she crying out for help? Was she a victim like myself in someone else's painting, trapped in someone else's vision?

I loved art as a young girl. My father went through a painting period. It's a beautiful form of expression. As a child, if there was a painting hung on a wall, I would bring it to life. I would give it a story and talk to the models. Their eyes would speak to me. They would always project feelings of happiness, contentment, darkness, or entrapment. I think those were the feelings I was having at the time.

This book is an accumulation of journal entries, moments of my life as I saw it with my own eyes. I used it as therapy to comfort me in times of frustration. I took all those emotions and released them from my head and put them down on paper so they wouldn't hurt me anymore. How grown-up I thought I was at eighteen. I had so much freedom yet trapped in someone else's world for half of my life. He painted a picture for everyone, and I was his model. How easy it was to make choices and how hard it was for me to walk away from those choices at such a young, influential age. I was a young Mona, and he was Leonardo.

I felt lost in my own home. His home. He painted this perfect picture of our family for the world to see that he was whole, but inside we were crumbling. It was always his painting, his dream, not mine.

There were days when desperation emerged like acid reflux in the back of my throat. I would swallow it down like a brave soldier and press on. But I was running out of time. God gave me this life to live and explore, and I was wasting it with a man I never loved. Why couldn't I just up and leave with three kids at my side? They deserve a happy home, and I deserve to be satisfied.

This book was a healing journey for me. It was a journey of love, forgiveness, and understanding to everyone in it. There's no blame cast upon the people in this book only observation and remembrance of past events and the emotions that surfaced from them which stifled my soul's ability to grow. But was I living? Is there a better version of me? Is this my awakening? I had so many questions over the years, but like most mothers, we put everyone's needs first. My time will come.

This is my story, through my eyes, looking out of his painting on 157 Elm Avenue.

I

CHAPTER ONE:
Trapped in his painting

*H*ave you ever felt trapped in life, in your mind, or just in a situation where you felt there was no way out? When the experience that you were living was not the life you wanted? You get a feeling in your gut that this is not the person for me, that there's someone else—a soulmate—but where is he? As you go through life, the days turned to weeks, months, and years. Where does the time go? You ask yourself, "How the hell did I get here?"

Maybe we, as women, allow our partners to paint us into a picture of how they see us, and that is how the world sees us. We let their perception of us to take over. Women of any age should not have to go through what I did—living with a partner who manipulates you with guilt and by using their unhappiness to beat you down. I was wearing someone else's shoes, but I didn't know who they were. I was trying to fit the part for everyone else but myself. Can I be the perfect wife, in this ideal family, trying to be the perfect daughter in the perfect home, to appease everyone but myself? Our life was full of imperfections hidden from the outside world. Blotches of paint scattered over a perfect picture for no one to see, as you never know what goes on behind closed doors. A true artist never reveals his or her work until completion.

This is my life and my experiences, how I got there, as best as I can remember them. I'm telling my story because I know there are women out there who are living a similar life. They try numerous times to wiggle their foot out of the bear trap, but that makes it worse. How do we get out?

We fill our days with friends and family but are emotionally empty and unsatisfied. My husband continuously told me—let's call him Leo—that I was a selfish person. How can that be? I'm the most selfless person I know. I sacrificed my entire life for him and our family. But at the time I didn't know anything about myself. I was young, and he was molding me like clay to be his trophy wife. Isn't it better to put your needs on the back burner and take care of everyone else first? I thought I was giving as much as I could to my family, but at the time, I was losing my own identity.

I was on an emotional roller coaster, and I needed to get off the ride! We can develop a Dr. Jekyll and Mr. Hyde personality split. We get trapped in believing our thoughts are real because they happened, so we acted out the present by living in the past. Our mind repeats events like a movie, but you think it's real-time. I didn't notice this until I was at the lowest point in my marriage. It took me twenty-four years to understand that I had become a product of my husband's emotional instability, or maybe it was mine. I didn't realize this until my children said, "Mom, you can leave now. Don't stay any longer for us. You and dad gave us an amazing start in life, now go and be happy." Wow, that was a big day for me! After I'd been put down for so long, my children reassured me that I had done an excellent job. Even my kids were witnessing my unraveling. I couldn't hide it any longer. I am no more crying in the shower. It was time to grow some steel balls and leave.

I'm telling my story so you can see how easy it was to become infatuated with an older man. As children, we start working our canvas, painting our own experiences on it as a work in progress. Some of us are fortunate to carry on with that picture until it's a beautiful painting of a life filled with many memories, traditions, and shared experiences. Then it's time for us to leave this realm and all it gave us.

For others, like myself, we meet someone and immediately leave our canvas behind. I was young. I didn't realize at the time, I left my life, my portrait, to be with him. Now I know, we start finger painting the day we are born. That handprint is ours until we reach an age where we start believing in other people's thoughts, your thoughts as to be real. We don't realize who influences our work until we are older and take time to reflect on it. I tried to dabble in my artwork, but I was always accommodating and pulled back into his picture.

I know there are women like me who have spent years running from the truth, with only glimpses of who they've become caught in passing in a mirror. I was a coward looking back at myself and wondering why I put up with the bullshit. Is it easier to stay? Embarrassing to leave? Do we sacrifice our own identities for our children? It felt like I was trapped in his painting.

I became Mona.

Why don't women leave a loveless marriage?

People will read this and say, "What is wrong with that woman, just leave, it's as simple as that." In my world and my mind, it wasn't that simple. For most, it isn't.

My mother use to say, "You married him. You must have loved him." I think now I loved the idea of him, an older man, not a boy. It was in my heart to love and respect him, but did I truly love him? When you are an 18-year-old girl, how do you know what you want and how do you see the difference? Maybe it was infatuation.

It's not that simple when you feel you have so much at stake. When you think you have so much to lose and will cause everyone so much disappointment. What binds us to these men?

Try walking in shoes with what feels like the weight of the world on your shoulders. Women like me live commitment, obligation, exhaustion, fear. I know why I stayed so long.

First, it was the guilt. Leo could dish out blame like it was candy to children, and every day was Halloween. He would say, "Why aren't you happy? Anyone would want this beautiful home, on this amazing piece of property." "You are selfish, Emily." In my mind, I would hear him speaking like Charlie Brown's teacher. "Wah, wah, wah, wah, wah, wah."

In my mind, I would say, "it's not the house, Leo; it's us; it's you." But for years I thought it was me. I had no real love to give.

His mother always said that my husband was a sweet baby, but that she spoiled him and created a monster. "He can be so stubborn." I'm guessing he always got his way. He was adopted, and I know now that it made a huge difference in our marriage. Maybe a sense of loss. They were incredible parents —loving and caring. What went wrong? Fear of abandonment, perhaps? He planted his roots in that house, but I was entangled in them, strangled by his insecurities, unable to grow myself.

The second reason for staying so long as the children, of course. I felt the need to protect them and keep them in their family home. How could I uproot them from the oasis he provided? The house had so many great memories under one roof. How could I make him sell this place? I would be the one leaving, and he would fight for full custody, calling me crazy. This was where my brainwashed mind was at the time. He made me feel guilty about that as well, always using that damn house as leverage. I knew he wasn't going anywhere, and it would have to be me. In the end, I gave up my emotional happiness to take care of my family and his.

The third reason was money. I wasn't financially independent. If I left now, could I have found an affordable place close to the kids' schools and be able to support myself, probably not? He had that chain of money insecurity wrapped around my ankle. That was my ball-and-chain. It was going to take some time, and in the end, after twenty-four years, I finally walked away from him, from that house, basically where I grew up.

If I hadn't, I would have been writing my autobiography from a jail cell.

"Honey, are you sure you don't want to blow dry your hair in the hot tub?"

2

CHAPTER TWO:

Where did I come from?

*L*et's go back to when I entered this world as Emily P. Zalott. My parents named me after my dad's birth mother. She passed away from complications a year after my dad was born in 1935. She was a remarkable woman, and I'm happy that my oldest looks like her. Sadly, my dad never had the chance to know her, but only to love the ghost of her. She's an angel for all of us. She was very intuitive and spiritual. She read palms and passed that gift on to my cousin. She returned to the spiritual realm so young.

My dad, Desi, was the baby of ten children. That alone would send me to my grave. I thought birthing three kids was a stretch, but ten? How did anyone survive with ten kids and no modern household appliances? And your body! How do you ever get that body back? Jane Fonda and her leg warming workouts were not around then. Maybe feeding and hand-washing laundry off a rock for eleven would burn those calories. My women's parts were never the same after three kids, never mind ten. The OBG gives your crotch a 6-week hiatus after giving birth. I would push that to 6 months and then bring the baby into bed with me to feed. My body was off-limits. I was the new milk-maid. I was a permanent cow until I said so. You try riding a bike after birthing three kids, and the bike seat is gone.

When I was a young girl, I would hear about the stories from the old country. I didn't understand what "the olden days" meant, until I saw my first episode of *Little House on the Prairie*, where Ma and Pa Ingalls ate, slept and bathed in the same room as their children, Laura, Mary, and Carrie. I loved Laura Ingalls. She was such a sweet apple pie country bumpkin with her braids, her petticoats, and her buckteeth with braces on. Wait a minute —they didn't have metal braces in those days. It didn't faze me at the time. Their living arrangements were a little tight, but life was much more straightforward. I hated that spoiled brat, Nellie Oleson. I wanted to cut her ringlets off and stab her with her peppermint stick. I was also jealous of her because her family's store was filled with all you can eat gumdrops and penny candy. I felt for the hardship of those Ingalls girls.

My dad was so poor; he chewed tar bubbles instead of gum. Tar bubbles? I love that in him. He would find them on the road, bubbling up on a sweltering hot summer day. His teeth are still perfect at eighty-four. I wonder if I should approach *Dragons' Den* with that one—Tar Bubble Gum. Ha!

Maybe that's why my father holds onto things so tight. He didn't have much. He appreciates what he does have.

The Grand Entrance

For my parents, Desi and Lucy, I was breakfast in bed that morning. It was Mother's Day, 1965. I came into the world as angry as hell. Some man was holding me by my ankles, and he just spanked me. What the hell was that for it just got here. Well, that set me off to six long months of crying. Maybe the masters made a mistake; my soul was in the wrong body, and I was screaming, but nobody was listening.

I was so different from my sister, and my nanny, Elphaba, Elle for short, though I belonged to another family at the hospital. She would say, "Lucy, you brought home the wrong baby. This baby is so ugly."

My grandmother would come to see us periodically and would often say, "Lucy, are you sure that's your baby. She's ugly and won't stop screaming?" I'm right here. I can hear you.

Okay, I was four days old at the time, but I have feelings too. Nanny was comparing me to my utterly adorable, plump, blonde, two-year-old sister, Lesley. I think that was the moment when my grandmother chose to love my sister more than me —way more. I must have sensed that even then.

I wasn't a noisy child. I was oblivious to the adult world. They did their thing; I did mine. I'm glad I had my make-believe world to play in. I didn't want that adult world ever. I guess I never was in any rush to grow-up. I tried to form my own opinions about life, not from the adult world but my world around me.

My sister Lesley and I have a great relationship now. We're two years apart and have mutual respect. I'm the baby of the family and my dad's favorite. I just added that because my sister will read this one day, and I want to see if she's paying attention. We always had our friends and activities, and we played and fought like typical sisters. I was still the pleaser. If my sister got into some mischief, I would say, "Dad, I'll cut the lawn for you," or "Mom, let me help you in the kitchen." If she missed her curfew, I would try to make it home early. I never slept, so when I would hear, "Here's Johnny," it was time to leave my room and lay in the hallway so I could watch Johnny Carson with mom.

Like most families in the 1970s, the children took care of the clean up after dinner. Dishwashers weren't available until a wonderful woman came around named Josephine Garis Cochrane of Shelbyville, Illinois. She invented and patented the first dishwasher on December 28, 1886. This wealthy woman, whose servants could not keep up with her entertaining, would break more dishes than she could handle. I think we should be celebrating Josephine Cochrane Day every year.

Lesley and I took turns washing and drying the dishes. One week I would wash, and she would dry. The next week we switched duties. The task turned into a bubble fight every night. My dad would walk by and bang our heads together to stop the bubble fiasco. That worked until the next night. Now I know why my memory is so bad. I'm glad we switched jobs each week so that the knocking was on the other side of the head. That helped put my brain back where it belonged.

We did one activity together: baton.

"Why?" I asked my mother.

"You'll love it," she replied.

I had no clue. My sister was good, but I was not. That thing hurt coming down from the sky after you tossed it! It was like a dull lawn dart. Why do people teach and take the baton? Unless you're a professional parade marcher, where would you use baton in life?

I'd practice outside in my parents' backyard —tossing, looking, and then running so I wouldn't get hit when it returned to earth. It was like a bloody weapon.

Soon the time came for the big show. I had a short pixie cut like Dorothy Hamill. I was my dad's boy, so I looked like the kid from the movie *Oliver*. We were in a Baton group for all ages.

There was my adorable sister, and her little brother, Oliver. We started our routine, and everything was going great. I was gaining confidence, and then it was time for the last toss. Just stick it, Oliver. I threw the baton into the air and moved into position. I was looking up with my hand in the air, waiting for the weapon to come back down, but instead, it landed right in the front row of the audience.

"Blasted, that sucked!"

I looked around; the crowd was laughing. I smiled to myself, that was funny. I didn't go back.

My sister and I did what most young ladies did in the seventies, Lesley joined Girl Guides, and I went off to Brownies. I figured any group that represented chocolate was right in my books. I had to wear an entire brown outfit, including a skirt. I looked like a chocolate chip cookie with a beret. I wasn't interested in cooking, sewing, or vacuuming. At the end of the course, if you were a high achiever, and your sash was full of badges, you would receive your wings to fly up to the Girl Guides, or you'd get your walking shoes. I got my walking shoes and did just that. Who needs Girl Guides?

3
CHAPTER THREE
Becoming My Father's Son

*M*y dad rescued me from all the things girls do. I became my dad's son at an early age. My mom lost a baby after I was born, a little boy. A medium once told me that Desi, my little brother, named after my dad, is with me always. That's comforting to know. I fell into the role of a tomboy quite comfortably. I think I already fitted the part plus I whirled around the yard like the Roadrunner. I had to burn off that energy somehow.

Christmas 1969, I asked for hockey equipment and received coal. The next Christmas I asked for nothing, I'm just going to get a hunk of coal again, I received hockey equipment. I started playing hockey mid-season at age six. I loved skating from the moment I first stepped onto the ice. There wasn't a massive contingent of girls playing then. We had to drive from city to city to look for female teams to play.

By the time I was twelve, I was traveling everywhere to play against other female teams. I was small and fast on the ice. I thought, *Cool, if I get good enough, I can play in the NHL like Daryl Sittler.* My dad stifled that when he told me girls could not play in the NHL. My god, what is this world coming too? I didn't realize until I reached puberty that I didn't belong on the ice with teenage boys. I mean, I belonged with adolescent boys, but not on the ice.

I continued to play hockey until I was forty. My daughters gave me pink skate guards for a joke one Christmas. I was in a co-ed league.

There was fur of us ladies sharing the changeroom. They looked like a biker gang in hockey equipment. One girl had a Foehawk hair-doo and Tattoos everywhere on her body. They scared the shit out of me. Is this UFC or hockey?

OMG I have my pink Terrycloth guards on my skates. I'm going to look like a princess. Once we were on the ice, I suddenly felt like Davey Keon. I could skate circles around them. Thanks, Dad.

You pass your thirties, after the child-rearing years, you need to cash your chest protector in for a longer one that ends at your bellybutton.

If God gave you a full set of hooters, you'd be tucking your zucchinis into your hockey pants.

I retired before that could happen.

Here's a tomboy moment. I had plenty of them with my pixie haircut. It didn't help matters. We moved when I was nine, leaving my friends behind. I started school in the middle of the school year, and it was awkward. I arrived at the principal's office, and he showed me around, then dropped me off where the girls were taking health education. I did a quick wave and sat in the back. The teacher said, "Excuse me, the boys are in the gym if you want to go join them." Who was she talking too? Me? Up I got to find the gym. The boys were playing dodgeball. It was meant to be. I met my future coach and mentored my entire fitness career. He became a friend until I graduated high school. Ken was the right mentor for me. I still remember his words: "Never let a ball drop." He named his daughter after me, Emily. I stayed with the boys that day in the gym, playing dodgeball. I was pretty damn good at it too. I found my top ten list of boyfriends in that class as well. Score!

That was an excellent time for my father and me. I was building a more personal bond with my dad beside a Father/Daughter one. Desi was a fantastic tap dancer. I wish he had stuck with it. I would have jumped into tap dancing. He belonged to a group that performed before the big bands would hit the stage. I think it would have been awesome to dance with him. I can see where my father had a taste for the stage and spent his life thirsting for that moment.

Timing is everything in life. For my father, Ricky, I think if it were a different time, a different family, he would have been an actor and a good one. When he was a boy in 1953, living in Niagara Falls, he got to meet Marilyn Monroe and Joseph Cotton when they were filming *Niagara*. I think he was star struck. He is full of life with a huge heart. My dad appears shy to people he doesn't know, but once you get to know him, he's fantastic. He played the department store Santa forever. I knew it was him. Now that's a role model. Who is better than Santa to a kid?

Desi is in his eighties now and spends all his free time at his Lions Club, raising money for sight-impaired people and fetching my mother's potatoes from the basement. I believe he and I are very similar people. My dad is a pleaser, like myself, and avoids confrontation. He also hates to rock the boat or cause a scene. For many years, he wouldn't even return something to the store if it were the wrong item. I'm not sure why … maybe it was embarrassing for him. He's better at it now. My mother, Lucy, *The Enforcer*, forces him to return things. She wears the balls and gives him the glory.

Do we turn into our parents? We have no choice. I do believe those personality traits are passed down from generation to generation. I am my father's daughter. My girlfriends have yelled at me more than once: "Emily, say no! You don't have to sign up for everything. If you join the PTA, we will kill you!" I'm not one of those moms. *Okay, I won't*, I'd think to myself. *What am I trying to prove here? I'll help somewhere else. I don't want to disappoint the kids.*

I worked four days a week, and I would help out at their school on my day off. There was always this unwritten competition between the working and non-working mothers at the school. The working moms already felt a pang of guilt, but then there was the notorious "Super Mom." This mother put us all to shame. She wore a cape that she made, of course. She flew around the entire school, cooking, baking, writing, sewing, crafting, coffee for the cross-guards, lunch with the principal. We all knew she was out of control. How could any of us keep up to her?

We didn't try. We let her run the show. We all have one at our children's school. It's their time to shine, let them.

I always believed if you decide to have children, you should stay home and raise them. I didn't do that. The life we were accustomed to required two incomes. Why do we do that to ourselves, so we don't lose our own identities? To keep up with the Jones'? Who is that family? I want to kill them all!

Women must be torn with that thought as well. Young mothers now have a year off with their child then return to work when that little creature morphs into a human being. I wanted to leave my firstborn at the hospital for the first year then pick her up.

A real people pleaser, by definition, is someone who believes they are worth less than others and who need to make up for what they are lacking, or think they lack. I don't think I feel that way about myself. There was a time when my profession defined me. At the time, I believed I required more education to be accepted with my peers. College wasn't good enough. Where did these feelings come from? My ex kept saying, "Go back to school if you want to be a physical education teacher." Then I realized that it's not what you do that defines you but how you do it, and you do it to the best of your ability. Years later I cleaned toilets for a living. They sparkled! Women were happy to come home to a clean house, and I was a big part of that.

When it comes to a pleaser in a personal relationship, they will frequently paint illusions that depict what they believe their partner wants to see, while never disclosing who and what they are. Maybe I never showed my true self because he wasn't the one to bring it out of me.

Who was I?

4

CHAPTER FOUR:

I wanted Movie Grandparents

*G*rowing up, I realized my mother and her mother had a strange relationship. My nanny was a little odd compared to some of my friends' grandparents. She wasn't in our lives much. Elle was a hard-working single woman from the old country, living in a big city, sewing uniforms and costumes to make ends meet. Who was my grandmother?

I lived in Dreamland, as a kid, I thought they were all the same—you know, the seniors that greeted you at the door, like in the movies, happy, bald, short, and smelling like Chantilly perfume.

I always loved Chevy Chase's *Christmas Vacation*. His children's we paint our grandparents into a perfect picture. They were loving, caring, sweet, odd little people. Why didn't my grandmother ever give me money or a handmade gift? Chevy's parents brought their grandchildren homemade gifts—a runny Jell-O mold or a cat wrapped up in a box for Christmas? I always wanted a greeting where they hug the shit out of you and kiss you with their coral lipstick, then slip you an envelope full of cash.

When I was a little girl, our family would visit my mother's Great Aunt and Uncle in Niagara-on-the-Lake. My aunt looked like a Russian nesting doll. And my Great Uncle Alex would node his toothless head in approval and say,"dah, dah" for yes, yes. As a kid, I would take one look at him and run away. My Great Aunt Stella had a life-sized doll, fully dressed in a 1970s pantsuit and matching hat. Every visit I'd dream of her giving me this doll on my way out the door. I didn't even like to play with dolls, but I was mesmerized with her moving eyes and long lashes. It never happened.

As I said, my grandmother didn't like me much, and she made it visible. Maybe I reminded her of someone that brought back emotions she didn't want to surface. Whatever it was, she was my only living grandparent. Beggars can't be choosers. We weren't close—she didn't know how to be. As the years passed, after she was gone, though, I developed a whole new respect for her. Life wasn't easy after the war. It was a time of building and regrouping. She lost her husband when my mom was seventeen, and some of her choices in life left her with guilt. Those feelings of guilt were never disclosed to us until her last dying day with my sister by her side. That's my mother's story for another time and another book.

Nanny would visit from Toronto periodically, and it was all about my sister. I still think she thought I belonged to another family. I felt like a visitor in my own home when she was around. I don't think she wanted to get to know me. I was the baby they brought home by mistake, as she said. It was as if she hated pets, and I was the family dog.

My sister would have beautiful gifts to open, and I would have my token box of Cadbury chocolate-covered finger cookies. It was like being enrolled in the jelly of the month club, but with my grandmother. I didn't notice at the time, as I was too busy being a kid—and I liked chocolate. I'd be outside running, climbing, biking, and just being a kid. I had no clue about the demons she faced daily or the skeletons that hung in her closet.

Until the day she died, she would look at me as if I was the adopted kid. I was a young woman in my teens, and she would say the darnedest things to me. She'd talk about meaningless topics, like the weather and her achy joints. She had an old European face, like a dried-up apple doll, and her fingers were gnarled with arthritis from years of being a seamstress. She smiled once in a while, and when she did, the dense cloud around her would evaporate. I decided at a young age that if and when I had my children, I would create memories between them and their grandparents—ones that they could pass on to their children.

I speak only of my nanny, as I only had one grandparent growing up. My dad's mother, Emily, passed away after he was born. My grandfather, her husband, passed when I was a young girl. When I think of him, I picture a large man. I'm sitting on his lap, and I can still smell the sweetness of his pipe. I believe he was one of the two friendly ghosts that sat in my piano room at 157 Elm Avenue. I enjoyed twenty-four years of that ghostly pipe smoke. It brought comfort to me like I was eight years old again.

My grandmother had some big hang-ups, and a guilty cloud with no silver lining hung over her head. She honestly couldn't be the parent or grandparent she wanted to be. There's a lesson in that: Always love and forgive yourself and others, and God will love and forgive you. Never live with guilt. It will consume you and eat you up like that man-eating plant in *Little Shop of Horrors*. "Feed Me!"

My parents moved Nanny from Toronto to a seniors' building close to our family, and later into a hospital—where your next stop is a bright, white light and the pearly gates with Saint Peter himself. "Tickets, please."

I tried to do my part, as my mother asked. "Go visit your grandmother; she won't be with us for much longer. Your university is right across the street." Nanny suffered from emphysema due to smoking her entire life. She inhaled a lifetime of nicotine. She was a lovely shade of yellow. She was on oxygen and still smoked as much as she could. Why not? I would roll her outside, and she would remind me to shut off her oxygen before I lit up her smoke. Now, given our non-history, you know exactly what was going through my mind—four, three, two, one, blast off! Her hospital sat at the top of a large hill. That wheelchair could pick up speeds of eighty kilometers an hour with a quick burst of O2. Runaway Nanny! Again, another pleasant daydream.

Her last words to me were so emotional—for her, anyway: "Emily, please lean closer so you can hear me. Here it comes. The moment she tells me how much she has loved me and will miss me when she is gone. "Emily, you shouldn't have bought another dog. Two dogs are two too many for your home. You can't even take care of yourself." My jaw dropped; my heart hit the floor.

That was warm and fuzzy? Okay then. Thank you and goodbye. See you on the other side!

I bent down, picked up my beating heart from the cold linoleum floor and walked out. *"Piss on you, Nana,"* I thought to myself. She waited another week to pass. My sister was flying home to see her one last time. I know they had an in-depth conversation about her guilt. I'm sure Saint Peter punched her ticket anyway.

5

CHAPTER FIVE

Family Dynamics

I come from a middle-class Canadian family of four living in a neighborhood in the 'burbs. As I said, my parents were a hardworking couple. They instilled a great work ethic in my sister and me. We'd do our chores around the house, and then it was off to pick fruit for the farmers. That was a blast. My father was amazing but very strict about swearing. He hated a potty mouth and still does. Oh and never hang up on your Mother, never!

We even had a swear jar. My mom would often mutter "bullshit," and that kept the jar filled.

One summer afternoon, I laid into my sister with a few choice words. My dad was outside, trimming our hedge. He perked up his ears, jumped over the bush like OJ Simpson hurdling those airport seats, and slapped the back of my leg. I had my father's handprint on the back of that leg for a week. I deserved it. There was no calling the cops on your parents in those days. We all got smacked for things, and most of the time, we deserved it.

There was an unspoken agreement in Zalott house. I never touch any of my dad's stuff without asking first. Ever. Our garage and basement were set up like a department store display area. He had shelves and shelves of neat and tidy items on them. Desi's profession was the stock manager for K-Mart, so the military order made sense. His garage is lined with corkboard, and all his tools, outlined with black Sharpie-marker like a body at a crime scene. If something was missing it, jumped at you the minute you walked into the room.

My mother, Lucy, was, and still is, a beautiful person inside and out. My cousin Suzy, who was at my parents' wedding, always says, "Your parents were a stunning couple, and your mom was a gorgeous bride." She still there for us and was also the boss of the house. Her weapon was her wooden spoon. If I were in trouble, she'd chase me around our bungalow, yelling, "Stop, Emily so that I can give you the spoon." I kept running, spewing out one-liners until she'd stop in exhaustion, laughing. I rarely got hit.

She went back to work when I started kindergarten. My mother was a nurse and a damn good one. She worked hard during the day as a nurse at a seniors' home. Her hard work paid off, and she became one of the directors by the time she retired. She treated the seniors with respect, giving them her full attention. Mom ran a pretty tight ship. I remember one time she required a ride home, and my dad brought me along to run in and get her. That was before cell phones.

Lucy worked in D Ward with patients with dementia and other ailments that caused their minds to fail them before their bodies. You could get into the ward, but you couldn't leave without a badge. I ran into the department to let my mother know we were waiting in the car for her. I was about eleven, and seeing those people rocking themselves or wandering the halls talking to themselves freaked me out. I just needed my mom, and I was trapped in a land of crazy older people. I was pinned to the wall when a woman came out of a room with her pantyhose around her knees, chasing me with a spoon and demanding tartar sauce. "Bring me tartar sauce! I want tartar sauce!" I ran to the exit door, but it didn't open. Splat! Down I went. That was one of my first experiences with an elderly person I didn't know. I thought m*y mother does this for a living. Why?* I've learned to appreciate the elderly, as I am slowly becoming one. In time I began to understand the elderly. They are people like you and me, in older bodies. They have created their work of art with life experiences and have amazing stories to tell. One day that will be me chasing some kid down a sterile hall, yelling for tartar sauce.

After work, my mother would complete her wifely errands, one of which was to collect my dad's addiction. No, not cocaine. Diet Pepsi. She'd look at the flyers and find out where it was on sale and then drive all over town to pick it up. She moved that stuff from shelf to cart, cart to bag, the bag to car, car to house, house to the basement. Thank God he poured his own drinks. My sister and I were not allowed Dad's pop! Other soda was not allowed in our home, but he was granted a shelf-full to tease us. As we got older, we would snag an entire bottle when we needed it for mix. He didn't count the bottles.

Our basement housed large glass containers (demijohns) of home-made wine, which on any given weekend were easy to siphon. Have you ever thrown-up homemade wine? It burns the nostril hairs coming back up. That all ended when one blew up. Our home stunk like a winery.

I now understand what it means when my mom says to my dad, "Desi, go get me some potatoes." That means, "I hauled your goddamn Pepsi for years, and now it's time for you to fetch me my potatoes for the rest of your life." They have a great marriage, but my mother is in control. My dad, like myself, was the pleaser, the "Yes, Dear" man. I understand now why she thought my ex was perfect for me: he was a lot like her. That works for some people, but it didn't work for me. It's all in the balance.

Lucy's ashes

Most cooks have a favorite spice. For my mother, her secret ingredient for most of her soups, stews, or whatever she was cooking, was cigarette ashes. Unintentional, of course. My father was deprived of real food growing up, so he made sure we ate home-cooking every night. Something, brown, white and beige. The beige was the cream corn out of the can, disgusting!

Mom always had a cigarette going. She was a light-it-and-leave-it smoker. My mother never really smoked them as much as she kept them burning between her lips, fingers, or in ashtrays. We had as many ashes as a crematorium. Our parents grew up with ads that told them smoking was sexy and cool, and if you weren't smoking, you were missing out. Their doctors smoked in their offices. Nobody knew then that it was going to cause an epidemic of cancers, or that second-hand smoke could kill you. Eating ashes probably wasn't suitable for anyone either.

Most parents would hotbox the family in the car. Cracking the windows wasn't enough. I hated them smoking. On long trips to the cottage, my sister would always get car sick and throw up in the back seat. Usually on me.

I would take my mother's cigarettes, remove half the tobacco, place a cardboard match inside, then pack the tobacco back in them. After a couple of long puffs…kaboom! The entire cigarette would be on fire. Did that stop her? Nope! I'd get the wooden spoon again.

Years later, I took my mom and oldest daughter, Alix to a local Tim Hortons coffee shop. This location had been chosen to have the first experimental glassed-in room for smokers. We grabbed our coffee, donut, or bagel and sat around the fishbowl, watching the people have a smoke ring contest. You couldn't see anyone in there. The smoke was so thick.

Alix said, "Mommy, what are those people doing in there?"

I replied, "Killing themselves, honey." What a strange world.

The new generation knows smoking can kill you, but my parents had no clue. They grew up with their doctors smoking in the office. My mom said, "That's never going to fly, an indoor smoking area at a donut shop." She was right: within a year, all smokers had to smoke outside any building in the food industry. My parents went cold turkey shortly after that, thank goodness.

The game of sorry!

A baby's first word in Canada should be "Sorry." Even before "Mama" and "Dada." We make our debut and immediately we're sorry for the inconvenience we caused everyone in the delivery room. I believe it comes from a lack of identity. Canada is known to be laid back and non-opinionated, so when we finally crawled out of our Igloos to something to say, we say it, then back down our aggressive tone by saying sorry. But are we?

I felt like Mama on the *Carol Burnett Show*. Mama was always ringing her little bell, yelling out, "Sorry." Why am I still sorry, for what, being here? I was still sorry: sorry in my home, sorry at work, and sorry on the street to strangers. I have a fear of people being angry with me or my actions. I can't let dead dogs lie, as they say. I need to know what I did so I can fix it as this can be the downfall of a pleaser. In a restaurant, I'll grab the waitress and apologize for not ordering lemon with my water. "Excuse me, sorry, hate to bother you, but when you're not busy, can you bring me some lemon for my water, please?"

On more than one occasion, I witnessed my mother being downright rude to waitresses on a few times. To the point where my sister and I would yell at her, "Be nice, Mom!" I was so embarrassed. Thankfully, she has mellowed in her old age.

The Canadian winter months are cold or damp, depending on your location. To beat the cold, we play hockey. We play in arenas or outside on the street or a pond. Failing that, we stay indoors and watch *Hockey Night in Canada*.

We had six channels growing up, which progressed to twelve if you had a Jerrold Starcom box to turn your antenna. I remember sitting on the living room floor with my sister when a lightning bolt traveled down the chimney and popped the knob right off the T.V.

I loved music reruns of *American Bandstand* and *Soul Train*. *The Brady Bunch* was big for us baby boomers growing up: "Marcia, Marcia, Marcia!" My sister liked *The Partridge Family* because David Cassidy was hot. Comedies were my favorite, like *Carol Burnett*, *I Love Lucy*, and *WKRP in Cincinnati*. Their Thanksgiving turkey giveaway was the best. The line of the year was, "As God is my witness, I thought turkeys could fly." That show made me laugh. I always wanted to escape into the television. I wanted to make people laugh.

As soon as we arrived home from school, we headed right back out to play. Parents let their kids play outside until the streetlights came on without the fear of strangers lurking in the dark shadows. We loved

Kick-the-can and Hide-and-go-seek. One late afternoon I was out playing street hockey in front of the house. There was always a game in progress. I got behind a slapshot and took it in the eyelid. It nearly popped my eye out. I ran into the house to get a cloth because my eye was on fire. My mom was cooking her usual mac and cheese with a sprinkle of ashes, please.

Mother the nurse, it was hard to find sympathy from Mom unless your bone was protruding from your skin. I had an open gash over my eye. Maybe one of Mom's butterfly Band-Aids will do the trick. I knew it must be gross when she told my dad to take me to the hospital because I needed stitches. *Wow, I'm going to the hospital. It must be serious.* Mom said, "Give her a piece of gum while the doctor sews her up." A piece of gum? What the hell's that going to do? Plug the wound? "Wait," I said. " I hate hospitals. Give me a sticky butterfly thing. It will go away". I hated hospitals. You could get sick from a hospital. There are so many germs. My sister had to spend a month in one once. I think I visited her three times. What rotten sister I was. But I didn't want to get sick.

We arrived at th*e germatorium's* emergency room, where the plastic surgeon was to meet us. My mom knew him well, so he was prompt to arrive. He said I got lucky, as I could have lost my eye had the stick gotten any closer. I thought to myself, *That's okay, my dad lost his sight in one eye when he was a young boy, and you'd never know it. Plus, you can have little jars of party pranks. Would you care for an eyeball cocktail?*

One night during a game of Hide-and-go-seek, we snuck into a friend's basement and hid behind the furnace. We thought it was a great spot. Suddenly, the brother comes flying down the basement stairs like a rag doll with the father in tow. We watched this boy get his ass kicked by his father. We were frozen; I couldn't move. We waited until they both left the basement, and then we hustled out as fast as we could. My first thought was, *Wow, and Franco must have done something awful to deserve a shit-kicking from his old man.* It never dawned on me to contact Family and Children Services, or even say something to my parents. That's just the way it was then.

As I mentioned before, ae typical family dinner in the '70s consisted of rubber meat, over boiled potato of some sort, and canned processed vegetables. It was all the same color: beige. I began playing with my food at a young age. I have a picture of me in a bowl of spaghetti and meatballs that I was wearing as a hat. My dad had had enough. I was being my stubborn self again and playing with my food. He acted quickly and dumped the entire bowl over my head. I deserved it.

Looking back now, my mom was an excellent cook—I didn't like food. I would play with it or even flush it down the toilet. I'd try to squeeze as many peas as I could into my cheeks like a squirrel gathering nuts, then ask to eave he table. I'd bend over the toilet and let those peas rip, shooting them out of my mouth like a gun. Mostly I survived on cereal, and peanut butter and jelly sandwiches and my mom's chocolate baking chips for cookies.

We could bring peanut butter to school in those days. What's an anaphylactic shock? There were no peanut allergies in the '70s—that we knew of—and the majority of kids went home for lunch. Yes, we ran home, shoved our sandwich down our throats, and ran back. If one of your classmates had an allergy, they ate at home or in the teacher's lounge. I don't remember kids having ADHD, Autism, Asperger's syndrome and the scariest of all Juvenile Diabetes. Where did we go wrong? Maybe it was all those canned vegetables we ate as kids.

Now the tables have turned. The "stay at home mother" is rare, and nobody heads home for lunch anymore. For our kids' school allowed students forty minutes to eat their lunch, and then go outside, get some fresh air. No balls, no running, and don't touch anything. There might be germs on the playground equipment. So basically, stand there and if you feel the need to move, stick your arms out and spin around until you fall-over. Ok, maybe I'm over exaggerating.

, There are so many playground rules enforced, so kids don't get hurt. Children always get hurt when playing; that's part of growing up. My middle daughter, Madison, was pushed into a tree in the playground. Ouch! The kids were playing. I didn't report anyone. I didn't go to that's child's home and punch the parent in the nose. The schools must police their activities, kids might get hurt, and then the parents will take it up with the principal and possibly sue the school board. It's a crazy life. I remember one principal telling my child that there would be no picking up snow. Really? What has this world come too?

I remember as a kid, walking by a teacher who was powerlifting a boy high above the lockers. He was being reprimanded for something he did. It was no big deal. I just kept walking. I knew it was none of business. He probably deserved it. Most kids are carpooled or bused to school. My kids walked until Grade Eight. Walking or biking is still the best form of transportation for anyone. Let them walk! We live in a very safe society. Why do we feel the need to instill fear into our parents and children?

6

Chapter Six:

Listen to your dreams

I was an over-imaginative child, even after I fell asleep. I think it comes from my very young terrible two-stage. I couldn't sleep so my mother would give me a facecloth, and I would hold it up against the wall, and I would bang my head to sleep. WTF was that all about? If that happened now to your child, the parent would take that kid to a shrink. That explains my Brain farts. I bruised my frontal lobe one too many times.

We all dream, some more than others. The secret is remembering your dreams. As a kid, I lived in a dreamland day and night. I dreamt of being on Broadway, running in the Olympics and flying. Have you ever imagined standing in the middle of your high school hallway, books in hand, and you can't find your class or get into your locker? I have, that's a nightmare. I have had a reoccurring dream since I was a little girl. It started as a nightmare, but now I'm never scared when it comes. In it, I'm being chased, and I stumble. I watch a wall of bricks fall on me. I become trapped under the rubble, unable to get up. I hover over my lifeless body. Each time I have this dream, I add to the story, like a movie or a book.

A man stands over me with his hand out. Maybe it's my angel. I've had that dream repeatedly

For years. If you study your dreams, you'll see that they all have meaning. Some indicate that your subconscious mind is trying to tell you something. Tony Crisp, author of *Dream Dictionary*, suggests that we all have dreams of being chased. And this might be your desire to escape from your fears or desires. I think he's right. That specific dream stopped immediately after my last cold night on the dock at the lake (more on that later).

Now I love falling asleep. Dreams are a gift, an escape from this life to the subconscious one. It's like being in a movie, or sometimes watching one. I can't wait to see what's in store for me. Just let my mind take over. Nowadays, my dreams are random. I've had dreams of helping people that were hurt, and I've had another recurring dream about a blonde girl. She was dead, like a walking zombie. She was standing on one side me, pointing at the hole. We were looking over a large construction pit with a crane and large construction vehicles around us. I'm not sure what that means. Was she buried there? I have also had souls come to me who were terrible in their human life. They screwed up badly and have come to me for answers. I'm tired of those dreams.

I wake up exhausted, wondering why I have to deal with these passed souls. Was I a horrible human being in a past life, and now I'm here to learn what I didn't last time? You need to be attentive to your dreams; they may contain the answers you are looking for. Leaving you a message or giving you a warning. If it's not in your dream, it could be in an object. Mine are dimes. I find them everywhere. Just the other day one fell from the sky, landing by my feet. A Canadian dime. I think it's my angels telling me I'm on the right track, or they're watching over me. It's comforting to know someone is watching out for you.

7

CHAPTER SEVEN:

The Mystery of the Mickey Mouse Watch

*H*ave you ever owned something so magical, so precious you never took it off? Or you had it tucked away in your box of treasures? I did. It was my Mickey Mouse Watch, straight from Disneyland. I wore that thing day and night. My mother would tell me to leave it in the box, so I would not lose it. Why have it if you can't wear it. That was my theory. You can't take it with you when you die unless you're buried in it. I still live that way. I use my china, burn my candles, and I never collect anything. Maybe running shoes. My mother was a collector of elephants. It had to stop. Our home was a mini safari.

Our middle school had a fantastic music teacher, Mr. Lawson. It was the seventies; the arts were considered a component of the school. We were doing a musical for our school production that year. I had to supply the props for the play. Mine was a pillow. I took my mom's goose down pillow from home. When the production was over, instead of taking it back home on my bike, I placed the pillow inside Mr. Lawson's piano. Was it a joke or was I too lazy to carry it back home? Both.

The following week in music class, the teacher sat at the bench, ready to play, when I remembered my pillow was in there. Odd, there was no noise coming from the piano. Mr. Lawson was stumped. I was smirking. He stood up, went around to the top, and opened it.

"Emily, is this your pillow?" "Yes, Sir," I replied. "Take-it-home," he said. He was smiling, so was the class. That's how I made people laugh.

During our Spring production, I heard Mr. Lawson yell, "Emily, you can't wear that watch during the Aboriginal portion of the play. They didn't wear Mickey Mouse watches in the outback of Australia."

How would he know that? I replied, "But I got it in Disneyland. It's a real Mickey Mouse watch, and his hands tell the time. I can't take it off. My mother said I'd lose it." Rehearsals were coming to an end. I was hoping Mr. Lawson forgot about my watch.

The curtain was about to open. I was twelve years old, standing center stage. I was in a brown burlap bag for a dress, shoe polish on my face, and a black curly wig. The music cued, and I started singing, "My boomerang won't come back." I was waving my boomerang all over the place while Mickey went tick, tick, tick. I still have the pictures. I'm telling you this story now because my mother was right. I did take that watch off, and I did lose it, like everything else I owned. I can hear her voice, "Emily if your head weren't attached, you would lose that too."

But magically it returned, thirty-six years later, with my knight in shining armor attached to it. Ask the universe, and you shall receive.

8

CHAPTER EIGHT:

A Little Girl and Her Magical Lake

*I*t's a known fact that if humans spend time around a body of water, they'll be happier and live longer. It makes sense. We're made up of water, we lived in a fluid for nine months before we entered this planet, and our ancestors came from the sea. Its' continually calling us back.

My dad's father, the tall cigar smoker, bought parcels of land after World War Two as an investment. He gave each of his children a piece of property on a beautiful spring-fed lake in northern Ontario. Since as far back as I can remember, I knew I was a lucky girl. Every summer was like a family reunion. This lake was magical. We all knew it. I found myself always looking up. I loved the sky, the clouds, the trees, everything God gave us to enjoy. I would wake every morning and thank him for another day in the woods amongst the trees. I'm not sure if it was our church that instilled these feelings in me, probably not. The only thing I remember about our church was my itchy clothes, tight dress shoes, and those white gloves. We all looked like Jackie O. The first time my parents took us up to the family lake, and I knew that if there was such a place called Heaven, I was in it. I remember wearing my running shoes in the lake for the first ten years of being there. The bottom of our pond was slimy. We called it Oggy-Bog. I loved the water, but I didn't need to know what was looming at the base, ready to get me.

The other memory that stands out from many is the sound of my Uncle's cement mixer. It ran a constant 15 hours a day. I'm not sure why. He could have turned our lake into a cement-bottom pool. I'm surprised nobody complained, I guess because we were all related.

If you're a cottager or camper, you have your memories, that provide that naturistic connection. The woods and water fill my soul, which brings me closer to the big guy.

Everything tastes better at the lake, and the air is so clean you sleep better. There are some memories stored in my head of the lake. Families are coming and going, constant visitors, days of floating in the lake. We lost my mother once. It wasn't a bad thing. Peaceful actually. Without any of us knowing, she decided to flip the dingy upside down and float on it in the bay. A wind picked up, and away she went. She was sleeping at the time. That woman could sleep through her alarm clock, a thunderstorm, and a house fire. We found her hours later, at the other end of the lake still sleeping.

One day I was on my dock meditating, ok I was hiding from the family, having a glass of wine ignoring the bullshit. I was struggling with emotional confusion and looking for answers and getting slow immersed in my self-pity when something amazing happened right in front of my eyes. A waterspout lifted itself thirty meters in the air. If you haven't witnessed one before, they look like a small tornado carrying water. It only lasted a minute, whirling right in front of my eyes. Then it just stopped, and the water that was funneled up into the air fell from the sky and rained on a portion of the lake. It was beautiful. Someone was listening to me. That was a sign of great magnitude.

My father loved us up there, but he was emotionally torn with the joy of us there and the mess we brought. He was fine as long as you didn't touch anything, and if you did, put it right back where you found it. Don't bring sand into the cottage or leave a wet towel on the ground. If that's, you can throw it in the garbage. It didn't make for a relaxing holiday with children. But this is how my dad was. I understand it's his cottage. He wanted you there, but don't ruffle any feathers. I remember when we put a family pool in our backyard. He said, "now you will never use the cottage." I replied, " Dad, of course, we will, we loved it up there. It's like he built it for everyone but on his terms. I remember watching my dad rake the beach smooth, smothering any memory of my girls being there. We weren't even out of the driveway. Heaven forbid you leave a sandcastle standing or an abandoned moat with water in it. I needed a holiday after we got home. That went on for years.

I know our lake has a magnetic pull to it; it draws you into its beauty. My sister recently told me that when she was six, she found herself sitting on our favorite rock at the lake, "Herbster-rock." She had an overwhelming feeling of peace. She felt like whatever happened in her life; she was going to be okay. I think she felt closer to God. It's a piece of heaven for all of us. Why can't we bring that feeling back home to the rat-race? My father is the only remaining child often. There are four cousins with permanent residences on our lake, and the rest are fair-weather travelers.

One late fall afternoon, my cousin's family cottage burnt to the ground. They went into town for supplies, and when they returned, it was gone. They wasted no time, and two years later they erected a family home and retired at the lake. Eight months later, only one full winter under their belt, my cousin died suddenly. It was devasting for all of us up there, but we realized John's exactly where he wants to be, on the lake. He's always with me now. That old saying, "here today gone tomorrow" becomes more profound when someone close to you passes suddenly. My cousin's ashes are in that lake. His son boats over to his dad's favorite spot every night after work and has a beer with him. Now that's special.

We are one with Nature

If you could paint your happiest memories on canvas what would your setting be? How old would you be? When I'm having a bad day, I would reach into my Rolodex of memories and bring my time at the cottage back to life when I was a young girl. I'm eight years, sitting in the highest mother spruce tree closest to God. Have you ever been to a friend's lake, or on your waterway, and felt one with nature? You have that urge to jump in a boat or a canoe and paddle out where the water is dead calm. You see a reflection of the shore in the water, and each stroke you take with the paddle creates tiny puddles that make a swirling pattern. You might even hear a loon or a blue heron, or a family of ducks. Those pictures are engraved in my mind.

I remember plenty of early morning rows with my partner, Roxy. It was glorious in the mornings. Life was waking up. We had a fish jump in the boat one time, and another time a beaver crossed our path, trying desperately to stop the water from moving. We had a swan elevate itself from the surface and fly right beside us at our speed. He turned and looked right at us. That was a moment I'll never forget. Now I bank those memories and carry them with me. I live every day with that calm, serene, blessed feeling. When we're younger, in the middle of life, raising kids, working and attempting to maintain some balance, we feel the need to pull ourselves out of that craziness and head to the lake, ocean, or the woods, where we can be one with nature. Allow ourselves that downtime we deserve. We deserve that time every day of our lives. We're here to enjoy life and what it has to offer.

I think it's called appreciation. We become so wrapped up in the daily grind that we forget who we are, why we're here, and what's important. That comes with maturity. If I only knew then what I know now about myself, I certainly wouldn't have sweated the small stuff. I picked up that little book, *Don't Sweat the Small Stuff*, and started reading it, but I was too busy to finish it. That's pathetic.

Samarah

When I was ten years old, my parents moved us across town during the school year. When you're a kid, a move across the City feels like a move across the country. I met my childhood girlfriend after the move. Samara was a blast. She had two much older brothers, so you could say, Samara was very mature for her age and suffered from shyness or anxiety. She taught me about grooming myself and becoming more feminine. Did you know you have to brush your hair a hundred times using a horsehair brush for it to shine? The problem is, we lose a hundred hairs a day, and I didn't have enough hair for that. One proper brushing and I'd be bald.

She also showed me how to pluck my eyebrows. One day she shaped them for me—poof, they were gone! I had no eyebrows when I got home. I tried to pencil them in, but Morticia Adams was starring me back in the mirror. They never grew back. Thank God for micro-blading and brow tattooing. Her mother was always laughing and had a cigarette in her hands, just like my mom, the same OCPD for both. There was always an older gentleman over, her best friend, Llyod. He still takes care of Donna. I remember playing her brother's albums in the living-room We must have played America's "Horse with no name," 1000 times over.

We were little devils together: jumping from her parents' roof into their cement pool and getting locked in the back of her dad's antique rumble seat. That was the start of my claustrophobia. We were in there for hours. Luckily, her dad was a cool guy. He taught us how to play basketball at the school and coached us for a few years after that. It wasn't until years later, as a grownup, I realized you never really know what goes on behind closed doors.

We were little pranksters at school as well. Once in Grade Six, we took a boy's bike and hid it in the orchard behind the school. At the end of the day when he came out for it, the bike was gone. Our prank turned into a robbery. Someone had taken his bicycle from the Orchard. We felt terrible. I wanted to apologize right then and there, but I was a coward. I didn't want to get in trouble. Now that I think about it, we were double trouble. The city set new boundaries for the middle schools, and we were separated for high school. The universe had my back on that one.

We both needed a new direction.

We are still great friends to this day, and we laugh about the past. You learn a lot from your past acquaintances. I do believe we were supposed to meet. We enriched each other's life at such a crucial age.

Karma comes full circle and bites me in the ass

Karma

By definition, the word "karma" means "action," not "fate." In Buddhism, karma is an energy created by willful action through thoughts, words, and deeds. We all create karma every minute, and the karma we create affects us. It's common to think of "my karma" as something you did in your last life that seals your fate in this life, but this is not the Buddhist under-standing. Karma is an action, and actions speak volumes. The future is not set in stone. You can change the course of your life right now by changing your voluntary (intentional) acts and self-destructive patterns.

I see now that what I did in a past life is my fate in this life. I came back to resolve, but did I? The lines, "you get what you deserve" and "careful what you wish for" hold a lot of truth.

"Karma's a bitch" as they say. It does come back to bite you in the butt. But it also allows your soul closure. One early morning I was running out to catch the recycling truck, and oh my god, the city worker resembled an over-grown Tyler Towne, the kid from Grade Six. Is this thboy, we played the bike prank?

Holy shit! Years evaporated right in front of my eyes. My guilty emo-tions came flooding back. Here's my chance to clear my conscience. I had to tell him it was us. My opportunity to set it straight, come clean, and free my smoldering guilt from twenty-five years ago. I took the entire blame. I blurted out the events that happened, even going back to the woods to retrieve his bike but it was,s already gone. That wasn't cool. I learned a huge lesson that day. You can't run from your fate.

The Truth about Karma and How to Use It as a Guiding Force .... https://buddhaimonia.com/blog/karma

9

CHAPTER NINE:

Lakepot

*T*hey built our high school on a busy street. They planted the auto body shop, the wood-working department, and all the tech shops in the smoking area on the side facing the road. That alone painted the wrong picture of our school.

I remember overhearing a friend's dad asked, "Why are we sending our kids to a school full of dirty, smoking delinquent, mechanics?" People would say, "It's just a trade school; they need an education."

Our high school was quite diverse. People from many facets of life came alive under that one roof. A good number of graduates became teachers who returned to the scene of the crime. The Catholic board was moving in on the city. Parents were busing their children across town to be with God. Public school didn't offer enough. We were a bad influence. Did we need direction from God?

Years later, our building was bought out by a Christian school board. The Christians came marching in. They slowly took over the school, one floor at a time, and our public school no longer existed.

My nickname was Little Zee in high school. Having an older sibling had its perks and pitfalls. I was always picked on by the older kids. I started as a minor and moved up the ranks. I honestly couldn't care less what they said or did to me. I was tiny, so tossing me into lockers and cupboards, squeezed between bleachers, and locked into change rooms wasn't a problem. I spent half a day in a Utility closet until a janitor heard me. To me, they were all a bunch of goofballs. Why would people want to hang with them? They tried too hard to be cool.

I was asked to pledge for my sister's sorority, Xi Upsilon Omega chapter. I honestly didn't understand the entire process, but if I could piss off these snobby girls and have some fun, I would. I honestly had no intention of becoming one of THEM. We carried fruit baskets around all day with an assortment of gadgets in them. I remember my pad of paper and pencil. I was written up often and made to do silly stunts if I was caught associating with boys. I never did get into that sorority, but I do remember a dark road, a farm, and throwing up raw eggs. Good times.

I was a pleaser by nature. I didn't have enemies, and I loved to make people laugh. I didn't do anything with a motive except to make that a person smile. In most cases, I was always the teacher's pet.

I remember my English teacher, Mr. M. He once mentioned that he loved sauerkraut. I brought one of my mom's mason jars of it to school for him one day: me, the pleaser. Okay, I could have used the extra marks. I often stopped to chat with my friends before the English class, and that day was no different. They were in the main bathroom before school started. I was telling a story, as usual, and swinging my plastic A&P bag, using my arms to speak. Suddenly, like a rocket, that mason jar of sauerkraut flew through the air towards the wall. I watched it in slow motion. My friend Karina acted swiftly, like Keanu Reeves dodging a bullet in *The Matrix*. I tried to catch it, but it smashed against the wall. That English teacher never got his sauerkraut, but if you ever want to clear a room fast, you now know what to do. That entire year, that bathroom had the aroma of Europe's Eastern bloc and a dog with stinky gas.

What's Pilates?????

Does the universe put you right where you need to be or is life a big coincidence? It is 1979, we had Physical Education every day and had to wear silly cotton blue rompers with our name embroidered on the back. We looked ridiculous. Maybe that was the point. Nobody stood out in the crowd. The boys in their oversized t-shirts and baggy shorts to conceal their random boners.

We had two female Phys. Ed. Teachers that our board of education paid. Boy, times have changed. I think they've taken a good part that out of our kids' high school curriculum. We had to have four Phys. Ed. Credits before we graduated, and I think now the high school kids only have to have one.

We had an archery room in the basement of our school, and one day our teacher took us all down there to learn a new movement class. I said to myself, *what a beautiful space to zone out and go to my happy place. This class is going to be engaging with that fancy word, Pilates.*

We were all lying on the floor, stretching, when the teacher said, "A man has developed a new form of stretching for your body. His name is Joseph Pilates. I think you might like it. I'm going to take you through some moves." That one class changed my life forever.

I realized that there was so much about the human body I didn't know. With all the sports I had done, I never thought about what my muscles do or where they were or what jobs they performed. It was a killer core class before the word CORE became common in the fitness world. I mention that because I've spent a lifetime teaching physical fitness and instructing women on how to build a stronger core to maintain good posture and physical balance. I see now how that introduction to Pilates changed my life.

So did the *Twenty Minute Workout* show. That was the first time I saw a workout for women on television, next to Jack LaLanne. It was three sexy women in tight uni suits and legwarmers. They were on a spinning pedestal. They could have strippers except they had clothes on.

I'm sure women of all ages tried doing this workout. I watched these women and followed their moves to this pathetic routine. They called it aerobics, but it was really for men if you know what I mean. Four more, three more, two more, one more, honestly so sexist!

There were also times in my high school life that I'm not very proud of. One was in Grade Nine Music class where we had in portables. Mrs. Schmidt was the music teacher. She was a tough cookie. There's no time for daydreaming in her class. We were learning a piece for the musical, and we had to sing it over and over. She was teaching us to sing from our diaphragm. She would walk around as we were holding a note she would punch each of us in the diaphragm. She was teaching us how to sit correctly and sing from our bellies.

Have you ever played out in your head what you wanted to say or do to a person? I don't know what got into me that day in the portable with Mrs. Schmidt. Maybe it was just a day of hormones. As she was showing us how to take a seat properly, she demonstrated. Right in front of me was an empty chair. In my mind, I hooked my foot under one of its legs. When she sat down, I would pull my leg towards me, and she would miss the chair. Now, remember, this was playing out in my mind, but what I didn't realize was that it was happening right in front of me.

I casually put my leg underneath the empty chair, and before I knew it, Mrs. Schmidt was on the floor. How did I go from a daydream to reality? I still hate myself for it. It wasn't funny when I saw her fall to the ground. She wasn't supposed to miss the chair, but there she was on the floor with her legs sprawled, dress pulled up. Adrenaline shot through me, my heart was in my throat, and my palms were all sweaty. I thought I was going to die, but instead of yelling, "I'm so sorry, Miss Schmidt," I heard my cowardly voice say, "Robyn, what did you do that for?" Did I do the chicken shit dance? My shame lasted two periods. I went out to the portable later that day and apologized. What kind of person was I? A pleaser would not do such a thing. She hated me from then on, and my mark dropped to 51 percent. She passed me, but barely.

Big lesson learned for a fifteen-year-old student. One, stop daydreaming in school; two, not everything is a joke, especially at another person's expense; and three, someone can lose an eye, as my mother would say.

CHAPTER TEN:

Jesus one, Emily zip

*M*y sister Left Me for Jesus. That's how I felt at the time. I was fifteen years old; I was finishing Grade Ten when my sister announced that after graduation, she was leaving with her boyfriend. They made their way out to Alberta, the land of frozen nostrils. Jesus was calling. My sister became a born-again Christian towards the end of high school. Her faith in God settled her down from her shenanigans, as my mom would say. One day she was throwing up in the back of a cop cruiser, and the next she was carrying her Bible everywhere, reciting verses and doing her devotions.

I missed her dearly. We were close, and she left at the age when sisters need each other. We had a landline and the writing of letters to communicate. It wasn't enough, there were days when I had so much to share and no big sister to share it. I know this now having three daughters of my own. Family is everything.

We would write letters back and forth. All of Lesley's letters ended in, "Love in Christ." I felt like the evil sister on the other side of the fence being judged by my Christian sister. "You must choose God as your savior," she would say. "You need to make a choice. Why do you not let Jesus in your heart and live through Him and with Him?" That's a loaded question for sixteen-year-old. I mean, we went to church as kids, but it had been a while since I thought about God that way. Isn't He everywhere anyway, including in my heart? Isn't it enough to spread the love to everyone, and yourself first, so you are capable of loving others? I had no answers for her.

My one and only sister had moved away for twenty-three years. That's a lot of time we missed. We grew apart and grew-up apart. I wanted us to enjoy our twenties together, raising our kids together, sister stuff. And believe me, I could have used her quite a bit in my twenties. One of the happiest days in my life, and for my parents as well, was when we found out she was returning with her husband and son.

My one and only nephew, Carson, Lesley's son, seemed like a picture to me. I didn't know him, he was blonde, adorable and looked like my middle daughter, Madison. Carson was a talented musician. By the age of five, you could see his potential. The few times I traveled out west to visit were the best holidays ever. I carried those memories back with me and cherished them until the next flight. He is a successful young man now, doing his Ph.D. at the University of Toronto. He will be a professor one day. I'm very proud of him.

The Break & Enter

It is still 1980, living with Ma and Pa Kettle. The Three Amigos. Slipping and sliding on my slippery canvas. I got caught breaking into my own home that year. My parents' neighbors were the Kravitz family from *The Bewitched Show*. Remember them? Gladys and Abner. We all have them. Gladys would stand in her front window and yell at her husband, Abner, about the things she saw happening. I think nowadays they call that "Neighbourhood Watch." I loved that show.

Glady's is the same woman that squealed on my sister and me for leaving the Desi's garge light on while my parents were away. Get a life, Gladys!

Well, it wasn't the first time I'd forgotten my house keys. It was after school, and I needed to get in, so I grabbed my dad's ladder and fired it up to the bathroom window on the second floor. I'm sure this is when Gladys saw me sliding into the house. I was making a sandwich when there was a knock at the door. It was a neighborhood police officer who wanted to know who I was and what I was doing in the house. I told him I lived there, and he said that the noisy, neighbor had seen someone climbing into the second-story window. I explained that I had forgotten my house key again and that the noisy neighbor had seen me entering my house. I had to show him a family photo to convince him. I mean, I was standing there in sweatpants eating leftovers. What robber would stick around and eat my mother's cooking?

Life was carefree in those days. High school was winding down for the year, and all was good. No drama. I had a boyfriend from another school. We had dated for two years, and it was time to move on, but being a pleaser, I didn't want to hurt him or for him to hate me. I have issues with disappointing people. Avoidance wasn't working. I had to do it face to face, which is the correct way to dump a person. We didn't have cell phones then. There was no sending a text with a sad face emoji attached to it. I drove over to his house, and while he was masked up and painting a car, I hollered over the noise of his compressor. "I don't want to see you anymore." Then I drove off. That went well. He only sat in front of my house for a week.

Most high school girls my age would rush home to watch Luke and Laura's romance unwind on *General Hospital*. There was no PVR or tape recording in my home. My parents were not jumping on the mainstream of technology. We had a VCR, but if you set it up to record, my parents would somehow turn off the timer. I wasn't interested in Luke and Laura or any other TV soaps. I had my sports and after school jobs. I preferred to make money. I don't think I was like most of the girls my age at school. I wasn't into gossip and local parties. I had an agenda, a plan—but what was it? Where does my painting begin?

I spent significant amounts of time in my room, sketching. My books were filled with pages of nature: blue skies, pine trees, forests, and birds. I always traced an image of me in those forests. Maybe that was my destiny, and I was subliminally guiding myself towards the woods.

II

CHAPTER ELEVEN:

Summer Jobs

*W*e all had them. Lucy would say, "Money doesn't grow on trees, you know." But fruit does. Growing up in Niagara, we knew we could make extra cash picking fruit. We'd take the city bus, or our parents would drop us off on a deserted road early in the morning. Farmers would arrive to take us to their fields or orchards. We picked cherries, peaches, strawberries, or whatever was in season. It was great while it lasted. By fifteen, I was ready for a real summer job, something where I could make some substantial coin. I didn't care how many hours I worked; I loved money, and my Chev-O-Matic piece of shit needed oil to run.

Pizzeria

"It's a pizzeria, for Christ's sake! Caress the dough, stop poking your fingers through it," the head cook would yell. Head Cook my ass. That kid was five years my senior. We had to do everything at the pizzeria, including flipping the dough while wearing a striped shirt and singing. Okay, I was the only one singing. I was pretty good at making pizza. I only put my finger through a few dough balls. One crazy Saturday during the dinner rush, our prep guy took ill and headed home. It was the boss's son, and he could do what he wanted—spoon-fed brat! We ran out of steak and cheese fixings, but I was on it. I grabbed the frozen steak from the freezer, fired up the meat slicer, and away I went. When I think back, I'm sure I put that safety down, but I guess not. Before I knew it, I was staring at the tip of my finger. It was sitting on a pile of frozen steak. Bloody hell. Not now! We were short-staffed and swamped, but I needed my finger.

Blood was oozing everywhere. I grabbed a rag, picked up the piece of my finger, put it back on like a puzzle piece, held my hand over my head, and yelled for help. I'm not sure why I knew what to do. Maybe it was my mother's hard-ass military tactics of nursing. I knew a butterfly bandage was not going to suffice, back to the Germatorium.

Our bodies know what to do in those situations. We go into shock so we can think straight, divert the pain. Anyway, someone drove me to the hospital, and they took me in right away. I looked at the waiting room full of late-night druggies, thinking, *they're going to have wait for their fix. I need a needle and thread.*

Lucy called her favorite plastic surgeon and met us there. The nurse was busy, and she had the bedside manner of a troll. I felt more like an inconvenience, but this was my finger we were talking about. Maybe she thought I was exaggerating, and it was just a papercut. She unwrapped the bloody towel from my hand, and the fingertip went flying across the floor like a piece of meat you throw to a dog.

My finger was not going to be mouse food. The nurse will have to get down on her hands and knees to find it. By this time, the shock was wearing off, and I was going to faint. The doctor arrived just in time to sew the fingertip back on. Okay, it wasn't my hand, only the tip of my finger but I lost a month of rowing training and decided that the pizzeria was not my calling on to the next crazy job.

Chantel's Seafood

My sister got me a job at the seafood restaurant in town. I was hired as the gopher. I was a short-order cook, dishwasher, and cleaning lady for the French owner. She would always yell, "Emily, what is your job tonight? What hat are you wearing?" in a thick Quebec accent. It still makes me smile. They were the oddest folks. One afternoon, the son took us out water skiing on the lake.

I had no clue that he was stoned. When it was my turn up on skis, I came out of the wake, and one ski got caught in a wave. It felt like I'd ripped my crotch open and given myself an instant douching. A boat pulled up to drag me on board, and as I was climbing up the ladder, my girlfriend told me to jump back into the water. I had lost my bikini top in the lake somewhere! That's a moment you don't forget when you're seventeen.

The owner's daughter, Charlotte, had epilepsy. She lived above the restaurant. She wasn't allowed to serve, just bus tables. On Saturday I watched her in the dining area. She was wearing a hockey helmet in case she had a seizure so that she wouldn't bang her head on a table. Well, she went down that night, plates and all. I recall her body squirming around on that black, and red lobster sculpted carpet. We just calmly kept working, stepping over her like she wasn't there. There was no cause for alarm. We had no cell phones, no pictures, no video not even a 911 call.

I did everything from doing the dishes to food prep. I'd open a can of snails, stuffed them back into their shells, slapped garlic butter on them, and cooked them so people could take them out of their shell and eat them — not my favorite. We had a full menu. There were the head cooks, and then there were the rest of us. We would cook up steaks, salmon steaks, lobsters, and crab with all the fixings.

One time I was trying to shuck oysters as fast as the orders were coming in, and I was getting cut up and frustrated. I'd had enough, so I tossed the oyster. It hit the freezer door and, voila, it opened. Time for my baseball skills to kick in! I threw enough oysters to pitch a nine-inning ball game.

On our break, we could sit outside with a plate food. My girlfriend would eat a plate of French fries. I took full advantage of my situation and often broiled up a salmon steak. We also enjoyed bringing our customers back to the lobster tanks. The rich, older gentlemen would come in with a pretty young woman on their arm. We'd allow the gentleman to climb up to the tank and pick his lobster. Most of the time they were afraid of the lobsters, so we'd have to reach in and choose the one they wanted. Yes, there were times when we got pinched—little bastards. After closing, my girlfriend and I would peel out of our smelly, seafood-crusted clothes and remove our Nike waffle trainers infused with lobster guts. My shoes were curled up at the toes like the ones on the wicked witch in *The Wizard of Oz* when the house lands on her. We'd douse ourselves with some body spray and head out for the night. I can imagine how we smelled. I know now that drunken sums have no sense of smell.

That reminds me of a joke my eighty-five-year-old father-in-law use to tell: "What did the blind man say when he walked past the fish market? Morning, ladies." He was legally blind, quirky, and hilarious. At that age, you can tell those jokes. I still miss him.

Mr. Smiley

It was a typical Saturday after work, and it was my girlfriend's turn to drive us over the river into Niagara Falls, New York. In those days, the price of gas was reasonable, so we'd all throw in fifty cents to fill the tank. We enjoyed the "drink and drown nights" the most. What seventeen-year-old would pass up all you can drink for five bucks? Kids these days think they invented Solo cups. We were filling them with any type of drink possible. We invented beer pong and headstand keg parties.

It wasn't long after we arrived at the bar we were approached by a couple of guys we didn't recognize from our hometown. They looked like they were having a fun night. The guy with wavy brown hair was cute and had a mischievous smile. His eyes sparkled, and I knew him into me. He was the kind of person you felt happy around. I felt this heaviness in my chest that I'd never felt before. He had what I would call the three L's: live long, love life, and laugh lots.

We chatted all night with the guys, who were from Toronto until the bar closed. We had plenty to drink and danced the night away. Then it was time to get back to our homeland. We showed them our favorite spot, The Flying Saucer restaurant, where Saucer Fries were to die for at three in the morning. Everything after 3:00 a.m. tasted awesome. Then we said our goodbyes, with no exchange of personal information of any kind. I'm not sure why I didn't ask for his contact information, which was his parents' house number. They drove off at sunrise back to the big city. It was only an hour away, but in those days, our friendship circles were small, and he and I traveled in different ones. We might as well have been from different planets. I didn't think we would see each other again. Little did I know that years later, the universe would throw that boy in front of me. (but more on that later).

Mugging

Weeks later, we found ourselves back over the river. I was hoping to run into the guys we'd met from out of town again. I dropped my two girl-friends off at the door and parked around the back behind the bar.

It wasn't long before a man started grabbing the strap of my purse from my shoulder. I wouldn't let go. There was valuable stuff in that bag. He pushed me down and said he had a gun and that I was to let go of my purse.

"Hell no, asshole," I said. We'd just had our graduation pictures developed, and all my friends' graduation pictures were in my bag.

I wasn't worried about my wallet, my ID, or the car keys … just my stupid grad pics. Photos were important to us then. I had collected all of my girlfriends' signed grad photos to put into my album, which I'd never got around to, so they were still in my purse. Damnit! There was niCloud back then. Once they were gone, they were gone.

I fought for my pictures, hoping my Jackie Chan fight moves would kick in. Finally, the strap broke off, and he ran away with everything. I found a police officer to walk with me through the streets, looking for my bag. He was a disgusting little man who made me feel uncomfortable, so I said, "Forget it." I felt safer with the guy who mugged me. I found my girlfriends, who were already half in the bag. They had no clue my life had been in danger or that we all had to find a ride home. Funny times.

The next day my dad had to drive me back to my car. That was a blessing in disguise. I realized what a dive the place was. My dad said,

"No, wonder you got mugged." I decided never to go back. Forget trying to find Mr. Smiley. As they say, that would be like trying to find a needle in a haystack.

I2

CHAPTER TWELVE:

My New Love: Rowing

*M*y love for sports never dissolved as I grew into my teens. I loved every minute of each Olympics, watching and wishing that was me. If I couldn't play in the NHL, I'd have to find a sport to satisfy my hunger. Summer arrived, and I was tired of baseball, it wasn't enough. Plus, if I had to watch my first base coach clean his ear out with a car key one more time, I was going to throw up — time for a sport where I could work hard and get results for myself.

They introduced Women's rowing first as an exhibition sport in 1947. By 1972 women's races became a permanent event. The rowing course was Dredged and redone for the 1999 World championships. Our High school didn't have a solid women's rowing team. There was no weight class for women's rowing at the time, and the distance was only a thousand meters. We had every shape and size in our boat, and we took last place in every race. I think if weren't for the ladies who chose to stop at the corner store for chips during the runs, we would have finished a race—and that meant individual athletes' butts needed to stay out of the tracks of the moving seat. Their asses did get stuck in the moving slide, creating a "butt jam" that caused that person to stop dead in their tracks. Often a rower would catch water and let go of their oar as it traveled over their head, making the oar act like an anchor for the moving boat. I had to find other girls like myself with the same mindset. Working out for some of our team was jogging to the corner store and walking back. That drove me nuts.

There was an actual high school team that would carry their coaches coach boat down to the dock for him. Those ladies scared the shit of me, but I was also jealous that I wasn't part of that team.

Summer rowing

One Saturday before work, I found myself down at the rowing club. I walked through the boathouse, feeling excited and a little scared. I could smell the athleticism. It was like being on a different planet. There was a familiarity that linger in the air.

Summer rowing takes on a whole new atmosphere. It's an older crowd, with more coaches and tons of athletes. It was very intimidating but exciting at the same time. Heading down to the launch dock, I passed through the boathouse and walked right by this good-looking guy washing his boat. I took note and moved on. There was eye candy everywhere. I knew I was going to like this place. Good looking rowers were coming and going, coaches' boats were heading out, and coxswains were busy instructing their athletes where to go. It was like a well-oiled machine, a symphony on water, and I was smitten.

The dock was busy with boats, oars, lip flops, piles of clothes, rowers, and coaches. It had the same atmosphere as high school spring rowing but to the next level of seriousness and competitiveness.

I might have a chance to make a summer boat. I recognized faces from the schoolboy regatta but knew only a few.

Stepping in a pile of goose shit with my flip flops, and slipping on the dock, I knew I was at one with nature. This place was calling me.

On my way out to where I dropped my bike, I found myself staring at the summer tryouts. Hmm, maybe I did have something to prove to myself. My high school rowing career sucked. I played every sport and made the volleyball, basketball, and track teams, but rowing was different. It was an individual sport emotionally as well as a team sport that tested your dedication, especially at 5:00 a.m. I had to learn discipline. It helped that the guys were cute.

I needed to redeem myself as an athlete, and summer rowing was calling my name. It was a world within itself. Besides testing your focus and ability, it allowed you to travel to some great cities and countries depending on your drive and determination. I've made the most amazing friendships with fellow rowers. My girlfriend, Clare, still heads up a masters rowing camp. She runs training camps, books regattas for the athletes and is the most amazing Coxwain. She can bring a rower up to their full potential. It's a gift. When I think of past races with her in the boat, it brings a smile to my face that I was privileged to share a boat with her and some most amazing athletes I will ever know. And I thank her for that. That was a lifetime ago. I enjoyed the sport for over thirty years until I had a huge set back with an accident (another story for later).

Right Place at the Right Time

You're at the right place at the right time when something good or great happens to you. That's the universe talking to you. For me, it was a job at a prominent sporting goods store. Saturdays were our busiest retail day. I remember working in the shoe department on Saturday. I was covering for an idiot who was cheating on his wife, right in the middle of the shoe department. When Nike said, "Just do it," I don't think they were referring to sex amongst the running shoes.

I didn't know he had a wife. You don't pay much attention to detail when you're a kid. In my eyes, he was just a douche-bag. Years later, I would end up working with that poor woman. She divorced him and moved on, thank goodness. It was an easy job selling sporting goods to non-athletic people. I wasn't on commission but loved sales anyway. That's where I met my future boss. He would shop in there often. He told me to go back to school and train for a job he had for me. It was a good job that allowed me to train, travel, and eventually spend time making babies—when the time was right. So that's what I did. I listened to this stranger, quit my job, left university, and started college. I changed my direction in life. Just like that. Why? It felt right. I loved getting up for work every day. I didn't feel like work I stayed with that man in his practice for over twenty-four years and loved every minute of it. Maybe we should rename WORK with PLAY, and then everyone will enjoy their job.

Fate or Destiny

I believe we have control over our destiny. Although the words "fate" and "destiny" mean similar things, to me, they're quite different. Fate puts opportunities right in front of us, but our destiny is ultimately determined by the decisions we make. For instance, if you go to a party and meet the perfect guy, that's fate. What you do about it is your destiny.

What was my destiny? I felt trapped and destined for a life of unhappiness if I didn't make a change. Nobodies fault but my own. You cant lay blame for your decisions. Was I doomed to live in someone else's happily ever after? How can you make someone happy if you are not satisfied inside?

I believe we're in full control of our choices and how we respond to what fate offers us, matters. We're here to learn lessons, and the hard decisions we must make to help us grow as humans. Our destiny isn't something we can sit by and let happen to us. We need to act on the opportunities presented to us. Fate may open doors, but our destiny allows us to walk through them.

Either we can let fate lead us through life, or we can shape our destiny. Take charge of your life, be responsible for you and only you. Stop living your life through past events and emotions, that's all they are, but the past. They are not the truth but mere perceptions. Why did I stay so long in an empty, emotionally bleak environment? I thought that was my destiny. Looking back,

I don't think I was acting like the person I was destined to be. I was trying to become the young wife he wanted, but he was not becoming the husband I wanted. What did I want?

We're all growing, learning, changing—that's part of our adventure. Maybe it was the guilt my husband cast upon all of us to live life through his eyes and not our own. We must speak up, stand our ground, and never let fear take over. Fate brought us together, but was he part of my destiny, is that what I wanted?

I love this quotation: *"The only person you are destined to become is the person you decide to be"* (Ralph Waldo Emerson).

13

CHAPTER THIRTEEN:
My Sista married Napoleon Dynamite

I was young, 18, I wasn't familiar with the wedding protocols. My sister Lesley was coming back home to marry her high school sweetheart, Sherman. The movie, Napoleon Dynamite didn't come out until 2004. Let's say my brother-in-law-to-be was Napoleon's doppelganger. Right down to the large gold-rimmed glasses. I remember the first time Lesley brought Napoleon home to our house. I mean, I saw Sherman at school, as a senior, but not in my kitchen, or sister's bedroom!

I wrote a poem about him; it went like this;

There once was a boy named Sherman,
when he was around, I could smell vermin.
His neck was made like a crane.
People said he was altogether,
but really, he was insane.
He met a girl, her head like a pearl,
Her hair soft and silky, his hair oily and milky.

Now if that's not profound writing what is?

My parents were thrilled that my sister was marrying Sherman, the boy she left town with to become a Baptist minister. It was the hottest day of the year. I remember it well as I had a race in the morning than her wedding in the afternoon. I wasn't a very helpful bridesmaid. I'm sure, at the time, she had me in her wedding party because I was family. I was not the type of girlfriend to jump in and make origami favors or cut flowers for bouquets.

"Just let me know where I need to be and what time." That was my involvement. We had the rehearsal the night before; it was great to see my sister again. We met at the church so we could rehearse. We were doing the dreaded wedding march down the aisle. I thought that was just in the movies, guess not. Tomorrow I get to do it for real. The wedding party is holding plastic shaped fans for a bouquet. Where did Lesley get her ideas from, a 1920's version of Weddings Are Us? Maybe this was Mary Pickford's idea. *Emily, you got this, I said to myself.*

The next day we woke up to 95-degree temperatures. 110 with humidity in the shade. Why would anyone marry in August? We went through the morning rituals of hair and make-up. I looked hideous with my 1980's Farrah hair and two-toned fuchsia taffeta dress. Try wearing taffeta in a 110-degree temps. Those pit stains will never come out. The church was hot. I was glad I was holding my plastic fan with fake flowers glued to it. Whatever breeze I can get, I will take. All of us were hot. The music cued. It was my turn to walk down the aisle holding onto my escort's arm. As we approached the six steps up to the altar, I realized I didn't have another hand to grab my long floor-length dress. Two steps up and the back of my heel poked through the taffeta. I first heard the rip of the dress before I fell flat on my face. I tripped my self up in that damn dress. I remember the arm I was holding, hoisted me back up to the standing position. I was still holding that fan. I could feel the sweat trickle down my legs, filling my pumps.

The crowd laughed.

Such a tomboy.

They just celebrated their 37th year of marital bliss. As blissful as any marriage.

14

Chapter Fourteen:

Our First Date

I was eighteen, and he was twenty-six when we met. I didn't realize there was such an age difference at the time. Eight years is not a big difference when you're in your thirties, but when a girl is still in her teens, with so much mental growing to do, I do believe the partner should be closer in age until your later years. It would not have been so intimidating. I first saw him washing his boat on my first trip to the rowing club. He was adorable, like a teddy bear, except for the nefarious mustache. I bugged him for years to shave that thing off. He was hiding behind it. Try kissing a man who has a small rug under his nose carrying the smells of his last five meals in it. YUK! I was in love with the idea of dating an athlete, especially a national team athlete. I was done with young men, the dating scene, girls my age, and partying. I might sound like I was 30 at the time, but mentally I was ready. I had plans. It was time to grow up. My transition phase had begun.

On our first date, Leo took me out as an adult. There was no nap needed before this date and no pre-drinking involved. It was only 7:00 p.m. We went to a local restaurant, not a bar. There was no cover charge or five-dollar all you can drink. There was an attendant in the bathroom offering me towelettes for my hands, and it smelled of flowers, not vomit. I could get used to this.

I sat across from him in a considerably large bamboo fan chair drinking my cocktail. I tried to savor it but sucked it back like a vampire on a bender. I took the swizzle stick and made an origami dragon out of it, expending my nervous energy through the straw. We made small talk and then he drove me home. I didn't see him again for a week or two. Remember, there was no social media and no cell phones; he had to find me at the rowing club to ask me out.

I saw him out at a bar with his buddies once, and he offered me a ride home. He was driving a two-seater sports car. His friend said I could sit on his lap. "Sure," I said. Seat belts were just an unused accessory at the time. We dropped his friend off and headed back to his house. It was late, and we were sitting at the kitchen table.

"Why are you whispering?" he asked at one point.

"I don't want to wake up your parents," I replied. I knew nothing personal about him yet.

He cracked up laughing. "My parents live in their place."

"I see. Well, thanks again. Time for me to go. The exit stage left. I'll walk," I said. This was all too much for me. As I was leaving, I thought, *Holy shit, he owns has his home, his car, and a full-time job. What the hell? I'm too young for all that shit.*

I can't remember when we started getting serious, but I do recall the night I popped in to see him. He introduced me to his roommate and his girlfriend. They seemed much older. How come I didn't see that then? They were on the floor, smoking a joint and playing Trivial Pursuit. I stood there feeling like a snot-nose kid, reeking of dead lobster (I just came from work). I had a choice. Head home, clean up, and meet my friends at the bar, or stay.

It was a pivotal moment for me. *I could have just turned on my heels and left for good, but something was stopping me.* Maybe it was time to grow up. I honestly can't remember. I know my parents were waiting for me to leave the roost so they could be empty nesters, but like that commercial, they kept serving cheese. I removed my smelly shoes, sat down on the floor, and joined in the game. And that was that — the beginning of a new life for me.

I was leaving university to start a new college program, quitting a couple of part-time jobs, and starting a full-time, five day a week career and rowing twice a day.

As time passed, our relationship grew. We had something in common—the importance of nutrition, respect for our powerful bodies, and enjoying outdoor activities— rowing must have been the common denominator. Why would any man want an unseasoned 18-year-old? Now that I'm older, I see that it was a stupid question.

I wasn't traveling in my circle anymore. I spent a good portion of my time at Leo's place away from Lucy and Ricky. I had no problem fitting into my new role. I became a character, a model, in his painting, his world. Maybe I took the easy way out in life and jumped onto his canvas?

1982 Baby Boomers

If you are born between 1944-1964, you are a baby-boomer. After WWII, the war vets arrived home, and the government supported these soldiers with a GI bill. Government-issued cash. They were given money in the bank and a roof over their heads. And in return, they created freedom and prosperity for years to come. They settled down with their sweethearts and started making babies. That's where we come in. I'm from the very end of that boom.

We graduated high school with a different mindset and fewer options then Millennials have today: college, university, or tech and trade schools. If that wasn't for you, there was work to be had and families to be made. We were living in a blue-collar town, so there was always factory work with a pension plan. Dating and marriage were simple too. If you were in a long-term relationship, then marriage and starting a family was the next step. There was no hesitation. You found the love of your life in high school or post-secondary education, then you moved in with them or married them. That's just the way it was, in my world, anyway.

I'm painting you this picture of the time and place we were living in. It was the '80s. There was no option to take a break, travel, or see the world before you were on to the next chapter of life. Not in my world unless you were in sport. The opportunity to move back in with our parents wasn't there. My parents stopped cooking with cheese years ago, meaning, there was nothing there for you. Your bedroom became a den or Mom's new sewing room.

You left, now make a life for yourself. That was it. It was a rarity to see any of your friends living with their parents after your schooling completed. I was jealous of Lesley and Napoleon, living the dream out west.

I'm thrilled to see young adults traveling after high school or university instead of finding full-time work and settling down. The world is grand, and there's plenty of time for the *"Leave it Beaver"* white picket fence lifestyle.

Hank - Mans' best friend

Time passed, and I was spending most of my free time at his place. We took the next step as most couples do and bought a dog. He was a big, beautiful mixed breed named Hank. He became the rowing club mascot. He'd hang around at the dock while we were out training. We loved him, and he became a bond between us.

Why can't we be more like dogs? They get upset like us and show their emotions, but minutes later they're back to their happy place with you. They don't keep that emotion burning, save that suffering moment for a later date.

Hank hated thunderstorms. We must have replaced our screen door twenty times because of that dog. One morning when Hank was outside, a storm was brewing in the distance. He was down the bank in the water, and I was still in bed. The next thing I knew, I got a phone call from my next-door neighbor, who had just moved into the neighborhood. She asked me what our dog's name was.

"Hank. Why?" I asked.

"Because he's lying in bed with me."

Oh no. My dog was about 120 pounds with long, blond hair—140 soaking wet. Hank looked like a person in a dog costume. When the storm came in, he ran up the bank and into the wrong house. He jumped through her screen door, ran upstairs, and leaped onto her bed. She woke up to a big, wet dog panting at the end of her bed. That cost us a screen door and new bedding.

Another event took place while driving home from Boston late one night in a Winnebago. A bunch of us were racing, and we decided to take a motorhome down for the weekend. We brought Hank with us, of course. It was about three o'clock in the morning, and I could hear the driver, a friend of ours, talking away and having this great conversation, but I didn't know who was still awake. When I popped my head towards the driver to see who was still up, I saw my dog, sitting in the passenger seat all buckled in. It was hilarious. He was friends with everyone. He's still with me. I saw a medium years ago, and she asked me, "Did you own a pet goat when you were younger?"

"No," I replied.

"Well, there's a large, hairy, white animal sitting right beside you. Your dog is with you always."

"OMG that's Hank," I said. He was my first real pet. My parents allowed us a turtle. A turtle and that was a stretch. It's comforting to know our pets stay with us forever. Maybe they are waiting at those pearly gates for us, waiting for us to crossover. There's that unconditional love we have for our pets. Whether you leave for 5 minutes or five days, you receive the same greeting at the door. I think I'm speaking for most of us who own pets. We would go out of our way for animals over humans any day. That has to say something for our society. In some countries, they eat those pets; it's called food.

15

CHAPTER FIFTEEN:

My Proposal

*N*ow that I look back, my entire relationship with Leo was odd. What was the next step in our relationship? Did I want to keep dating, maybe live together or did I want more? Did Leo want more? It was the eighties. Everyone around us was getting married. We had a few years under our belt and a dog. Now, do we tie the knot? I was waiting for a ring. I thought that was next. Maybe it would be on my birthday or Christmas. Three years passed, and there was nothing. We were out walking the dog once when I said to him, "Are we going to date forever or turn this into something more?"

"Are you sure you want to get married?" he asked.

"Sure." That was about as exciting as a hangnail, but that was my romantic proposal, and I accepted. We just fell into it. I was in love with the idea of marriage, taking the next step towards happiness. I was done partying with my friends, and I fit in excellent with his rowing crowd.

His mother gave him her mother's ring to pass on to me. It was an antique and very sweet; it also came with the last batch of pie crust she was rolling. He never had it cleaned. He always complained about how much things cost, so I didn't want to ask him for a brand-new ring. *That would be selfish of me, would it?* I would accept this one. Maybe over time, he would present me with my very own ring.

I should have spoken up, but he was a bit cheap, and a ring would cost money. We had bills and significant property taxes to pay. Why not put the cost of a ring into something constructive, like renovations? Bloody house Renos...

Why didn't I speak up? That might have changed everything or caused a huge argument. Selfish Emily. I should have said something sooner. How would have Leo known this bothered me for years. Expectations are fine and dandy, but if you don't have any, you are never disappointed, or are you?

There were so many little red flags, and I missed them all. I thought maybe Leo would surprise me with my ring in the future, perhaps after our first child. But the funds were spent on more Renos for the house. One year I got a driveway poured, then an addition and a covered porch. Oh, and one year I asked for a road bike to cycle with the Sunflowers, a local women's cycling group. Instead, I received a hot tub. I think that was for him. Was that my fault, again I didn't speak up? You should never assume someone knows what you're thinking, just because you live together.

Night-School for non-Catholic's

I still remember it like it was yesterday. Our wedding was going to be held in September. It felt like it only took a few phone calls to book everything. Maybe that was my first clue. It was too easy. Did I not care much? It may have been my immaturity or my lack of love for him, and I'm not sure. I know how I feel now, and it was not how I felt then. I wasn't marrying the man I was supposed to be with. It felt surreal and temporary. I didn't feel that rush of adrenaline I should have felt. Did I have cold feet? Is that what I was feeling? You only get that knowledge with age and experience. I never had that warm, fuzzy feeling people get when they're with that particular person like they can't live without them, that nervous energy that shoots through your body.

At the time, I was marrying my best friend, the guy I hung out with, a roommate. I thought that's how you were supposed to feel about your future husband. Instead, I turned him into my bossy older brother — another red flag.

We had to get married in a Catholic church. My fiancé was Catholic, so it seemed like the thing to do, primarily if we intended to send our future children to a Catholic school. To be allowed to do so, I had to attend classes with my fiancé and the priest. I still don't understand how a man who isn't allowed to marry or have kids is qualified to give you classes on marriage. And what's with no birth control?

I was very uncomfortable. I was twenty-one and the priest, although a lovely man, made me feel uncomfortable. I had questions for him. Why do we have single priests counsel couples? What real-life experience do they have? I chose to sit quietly and nod through these sessions. After a month with Father Peter, he permitted us to marry in his church. I think he just wanted to get rid of me. Years later, it was me gathering the kids for church service. I thought it was essential to be part of our community. Leo kept saying, "I am a good Christian. I don't have to go to church to prove it." I would reply, "It's not about you, we have children, it should be essential to us. I guess that didn't matter. Now I realize Catholics have enough bench time for ten lifetimes.

The Royal Wedding

I called my wedding a Royal Wedding. Wasn't Lady Diana much younger than Charles? We were in very similar spaces, minus the money. I think we were both a bit lost and out of place. I used to think she looked as unhappy as I felt. Her death still haunts me. It was a sad day for everyone, and another red flag for me, maybe?

We'd just finished the rowing championships, and we'd live in ballcaps. I just needed a change. I chopped my hair off, and I did look like Lady Diana. That wasn't on purpose. My mother was furious with me. She immediately took me out to return my baby's breath clip to buy a hat to cover up my haircut. I don't know why I didn't argue the point. The hat looked like a lacy sombrero next to my peanut-sized head. Remember, it was the '80s: big hair and itchy dresses with puffy sleeves. I looked like a table doily with a Mexican hat for a centerpiece.

Was the universe talking to me?

The day before the wedding, my mother's sleeve of her "Mother of the bride" dress stuck to the iron. I went into work for my shift, and I was cleaning out my sink when Comet cleaner splashed up into both my eyes. They were red and itchy until the wedding. Why was I at work the day before my wedding? Did I not have things to do? The morning of the wedding, my hairdresser forgot to schedule my wedding party for hair appointments, she was fully booked up. Of course, she was. I dispersed my wedding party downtown to random salons to get their hair done. If you're a woman, your hair is a significant part of you, but it's especially important when it comes to an occasion where pictures have to be perfect. When they were finished, they looked like an all-girls country-western band.

Our priest was called away for a family emergency, so we had another priest fill in. Honestly, why hadn't I thrown in the towel yet? So many signs. He was an odd, older gentleman with a certain way about him. After a few words, he would hiccup or gasp for air. I wasn't sure what it was. He would speak and pause, and I thought it was my turn to speak. Eye contact and hand gestures led the entire ceremony.

The church was packed, and it was hot. I was sweating under my sombrero. It was standing room only, and there was a lot of snickering throughout the service. The priest hiccupped and gasped for air the entire time. It echoed throughout the church. I signed the marriage certificate and held it up like I'd won a lottery. If I only knew what I was getting into. But after the line "'til death do you part," my married life began, and my own identity ended. Why do they have to use that line? It's so final. Why not," here's to a happy beginning and a lifetime of marital bliss." I forgot Catholics love misery.

After pictures, our limo broke down on the highway on the way back to the reception. Not one person stopped to give a ride to a girl in a long, white, flowing dress. Really? Maybe they didn't like my hat. Perhaps I should have been looking for that horse to ride away into the sunset. In the end, the wedding was a blast. Maybe we should have had the party, and the gifts, without the ceremony. It was the year of crystal. I received six crystal salad bowls, five vases, and 110 wine glasses. Did I not have a bridal registry at Robinsons?

16

CHAPTER SIXTEEN:

The Money Pit

*H*e bought the house from his parents a year before I met him. They gave him a head start in life. His parents were good people. I think sometimes he forgets where he came from and what his parents did for him. When I met Leo, the house was a smelly old dump. People living in the rooms upstairs, laundry machines in the kitchen, which by looking at the linoleum floor, overflowed more than once. The flooring was dated, old carpeting is worn out in the middle where people have carved a path for decades. Do you remember the movie, *The Money Pit*, Well I'm Goldie Hawn, accept I'm doing my part. The house was a century-old and needed updating badly. I came into the picture the time when it was time to shut down the party house.

I'm painting you this picture to show you how involved I was in this house, right from the beginning. If he wanted work done, I was the girl to go it. Leo was on a budget. We only hired out for the big jobs never for anything cosmetic. We ripped out carpets and painted walls, windows, and ceilings right down to the lathe. My dad and I stripped wood and painted fences to keep down costs. I remember being eight months pregnant, still ripping out hallway walls. It became a joke on our busy street. It was like I was filming a Benjamin Moore commercial. We lived on a busy street when friends drove by. I would wave my brush or heat gun in the air. It felt good to keep working. Do my share.

He was always in control, but in a pleasant way. We fell into our roles nicely. However, early on in our marriage, if we ever argued, he would say, "Just leave." Why would I leave if we were disagreeing? This is where I live, and it's my home, too. It was strange. I watched him morph into someone else. It didn't feel right, and I didn't understand at the time. He made me feel like I wasn't welcome, a bit insecure about my role here. I just knew we were not; good at arguing. Lucy and Desi had marital spats all the time but ended with a kiss. That was the norm in my home. I learned to avoid conflict with him. I sure as hell wasn't leaving. That's an odd thing to say. Where would I go, and why would I leave? I may not have contributed equally monetarily, but I did in every other way.

He was stubborn, non-confrontational, and a shitty arguer. I think more couples would still be together if they learned to sort out our differences. Agree to disagree. It's essential to get it out and move on. I felt like it was his way or the highway. If you have something to say, say it, be done with it, and move on. Not every argument ends in divorce.

Leo was very insecure with me, or maybe I with him. I was always walking on eggshells with him. It didn't matter where we went. I'd be in trouble once we were leaving and I got in the car. He'd say, "I saw you looking at that guy or "I saw that guy looking at you." He made it sound like I was flirting. He was a very suspicious person. I never put myself out there. I was just me happy, laughing, and enjoying myself. But to him, it was flirtatious and caused the problems — another big red flag.

Throughout this time, I had a constant ache in my chest. I was trying to fill a void where my heart should have been. The clue was loneliness. We had a parent-daughter relationship, and it wasn't working for me. I never felt like his equal. He was the boss, and I was his employee. Maybe I was too young for this gig. I kept trying.

One day when I got home from work, I found him with my Visa bill. Again just starting in our marriage. He asked me for my credit card and said I had to watch my spending. I was an adult and working, and it was my credit card. Why would he open my mail? We never had a joint account. We just fell into a pattern. He continued to do the banking, and I paid for incidentals.

I think he feared I would put us into debt. Or he needed to have control over what was going in and going out. I know I wouldn't have; I was very good with my money.

I feel money is the root of all evil. It causes stress in people and marriages — the mighty old dollar in general causes more arguments and break-ups in relationships. Financial counseling is what couples require not Catholic night-school for brides-to-be.

17

CHAPTER SEVENTEEN:

Stop this ride I'm getting off!

*T*ime passed on the home front. We had the white picket fence, the token dog, and we were always working on the house. My gut was still telling me to run! Something wasn't right. We weren't right. It's like buying a pair of shoes: you get them home, try them on, and discover that they're two different sizes. They looked perfect on the shelf but not on your feet.

We were painting the perfect picture for everyone to see. What was that all about? I came home from work one day, and my mail was open again. "Emily, you are overspending," he yelled. "You need to budget yourself better." Still about money. I know this was just his observation and interpretation. But I felt like his daughter getting reprimanded. How does one person start acting like an adult, when they are being treated like a child?

I replied in my head, "Yes, Dad."

What the fuck was he talking about? I was very good with my money. I bought my first car at sixteen. I worked every job you could think of to build a little nest egg. Plus, this was my account, my business.

Why was I panicking? I started to think that maybe this wasn't my prince coming to save the day. I knew my life with him was going to be overwhelming, as I'm not about money and I don't need a big, expensive house. We both worked middle-income jobs, and the taxes living on the water were crazy. I thought that maybe I had made a mistake. The only thing I knew was that I had to get out before it was too late.

Too late for what? What the hell was wrong with me? I thought I'd had the perfect life so far. My mother told me that I should be happy and grateful. My married friends were content, and I should have been too. But I kept thinking of our wedding vows and that line about, 'til death do us part! I plan to live a very long life, so waiting until my death won't cut it. I needed to leave immediately.

Mother Knows Best?

Anytime I complained to my mother, and she would say that it was utterly ordinary, followed by a "now listen, Emily" speech. So, I never did tell my parents what I was about to do, leave Leo until it was over. I couldn't bear to see my mother's disappointed face as she pronounced my full name, syllable by syllable when I told her I wasn't happy and was leaving him. "E-M-I-LY P Z-A-L-O-T-T. You haven't given this marriage enough time and effort even to know what you want."

Maybe I hadn't. Perhaps I was selfish. *It's my life, for goodness sake.* She would then say, "You're going to have your down periods in your relationship. I had them with your father." *But we're talking about me, Mom, and my feelings. Don't they matter? Leo and I are only in the first two years. Something doesn't feel right.*

My mom was a very matter-of-fact person. She wore everything, good or bad, on her sleeve. "You make your bed, and you lay in it," she said. When I finally told my mom in confidence that I was leaving, taking a break, she said, "You need to give your marriage time. Why did you get married in the first place if you didn't love him? What's wrong with you? You have a loving, supporting, (emotionally strangling) husband with a good solid job and a beautiful home. He's a good provider. You can't leave without really trying." I didn't want to hear any of that. That's not what I needed to hear. I'm not blaming her; I was looking for her support. I was hearing Charlie Brown's teacher again, Wah Wah Wah! So, I left. That didn't go so well. Years later, my daughter was in the same situation. I gave her different advice and a horse to ride away into the sunset.

I decided to ignore what she said, listen to my gut instinct and use Forrest Gump's girlfriend Jenny's advice: RUN, EMILY, RUN. And I did. I ran right to my girlfriend's parents' basement.

Lady Diana was killed in a tragic automobile accident a week later, August 31, 1997. A piece of me died with her.

Money doesn't grow on a tree!

I didn't realize this until later in life, my mother, unintentionally, instilled the fear of never having enough money into my brain. That you need money to survive, that the all mighty dollar measures your self-worth. You need to be able to support yourself if something happens. Like I leave my husband. But it's not. I measure my life in the happiness meter. My cup is always half full, never half empty.

To her, I felt like my success was measured in my paycheck, in what I was making and how I was planning my retirement. Desi and Lucy come from a generation of smart money-conscious people. They spent within their means. They never racked up huge credit card debt or felt the need to own a million-dollar home they couldn't afford. That age group was smart with their money. They planned for their retirement. Their employer offered pension plans. I did learn a lot from Lucy.

Years later, I re-purchased, *The Wealthy Barber*. I gave a copy to each of my daughters. His theory is, after each paycheck, you pay yourself first, well after our government takes half. It works, a small forced savings account. MAD money. Are you insane? Who's kidding who? There's never enough money when it comes to raising kids. Whoever said, *Money's not everything*, must have been broke. The sad thing is; currently, you do need a certain amount to survive. The Government takes half our paycheck, taxes our property, food, clothing, gas. If you have a mortgage, you better make enough to put your monthly payment on the primciple. For myself, I can only pay the minimun, which covers the interest. That is not a healthy stress-free way to live. Someone is getting rich, and it isn't the little people.

My mom still harps on me about my retirement and will I have enough. Who's retiring? Shes outlived her pension, meaning, The longer you stay alive, it keeps paying out. She's very proud of this fact.It's like living on fun money.It also makes me feel bad about myself when she boosts about it. This generation, without a pension or a considerable nest egg, no one is retiring unless you invested well or bought property.

My mother has a Rummoli game once a month with her friends. She keeps a drawer filled with every nickel she has won from 1980. That drawer was filled with zippy bags of winnings. Nickels. This is the same woman that quit smoking years ago and still saves her monthly output that she would have spent on smokes. My parents collect their toonies and loonies for trips they never take. And don't ask to borrow some change, they won't have any. She would say," Emily, that's for our holiday." Like they would have to cancel their trip because I borrowed ten dollars in toonies. Ut, this is the mindset of that generation. They are saving for a rainy day.

If you were ever caught unscrewing the plexiglass cover on the wood elephant bank and removing some change, you would have your hand cut off to the elbow with my father's jigsaw, put it back where it belongs, in the garage where the black outline is.

And now that we are on that topic, what Canadians came up with the idea of calling our money toonies and loonies. No wonder Americans think we are allegedly addicted to maple syrup and fishing. So, this is being Canadian.

18

CHAPTER EIGHTEEN:

Girl in their basement

*A*fter two years of marriage and a speech from my mother, I drove home from work like it was any other day. I pulled into the driveway and saw that Leo was outside repairing our piece of shit fence. I walked by my husband, went upstairs, packed my suitcase, and left just like that. I felt if I didn't do it now, I wouldn't ever leave.

I started living in my girlfriend's basement since my parents' home was not an option. I think about it now, those people took me in and let me stay, shirk my responsibilities to life, and sponge off them for months. This is a choice I made, and I had to act like a grown-up, and bloody well find myself. Plus, I couldn't face the disappointment of both my parents every day after a failed marriage. I know my girlfriend's parents would not judge me, love, and accept me. I was the Trole in their basement, stay as long as you'd like

It was a strange time for me. I was working and still training, but now living with a bit of freedom. I was twenty-three years old, for goodness sake! I was bloody happy not to be around him and that house. My girlfriend and I had a great time acting our age: working during the day and going out on the weekends. Those 3:00 a.m. homemade Chef Boyardee pizzas were excellent while we laughed, sang, and danced to Much Music. I was just a kid again, and Leo wasn't watching my every move. I felt free. What's wrong with that, except I had that *"Until death do you part,'* commitment hanging over my head.

I would lunch with my Mother's sister, Elizabeth, at least once a week. She didn't have children of her own and loved my sister and me dearly. She worked in the town she lived in. Liz would say to me, "Emily, you need to be sure this is what you want. All marriages have their ups and downs." She said those exact words to me again twenty-three years later before she passed away. I still think of her often. A medium told me once that Betty was my guardian angel. She leaves me dimes whenever she's around. I have quite a collection to remember her by.

Leo was very persistent at making the marriage work. I suggested the marriage counselor. The honeymoon was over, and reality was setting in. I figured I had two choices: I find a little apartment for myself, or do I go back to Leo? I can't go home to Lucy.

We met in the marriage counselor's parking lot. I wanted this stranger to give me some answers. He was a professional. I couldn't decide on my own, as too much was at stake. Everyone's happiness was riding on my decision. I couldn't disappoint everyone, could I? The world was depending on me! Well, that's how I felt. We spent all the money on that one particular day, and I'm going to destroy that for my own happiness?

We sat on the couch beside each other, and the counselor asked us some basic questions about how we met, how long we dated, and when we married. I found myself daydreaming. I do my best work in my happy place. *Self, you need to be a better listener.* I thought to myself.

Out of nowhere, in my mind, I was transported to another place. I was a contestant on the game show *Jeopardy*, and the counselor was Alex Trebek. He'd just asked me the million-dollar question. "Emily, found in a situation where you had to move out of your friend's basement, where would you go?" They cued the music while I thought of the correct answer. "Your answer to all the money, Emily." My time was up! I blinked and was back from my happy place. "Back to Leo, Alex." Did I say that? Snap out of it, Emily.

"Pardon me? I didn't hear you."

I was back in the office, on the couch with Leo.

"Leo wants you back," he repeated, "but you both need to do some homework so that this marriage will work."

This man doesn't know us, like I wasn't doing my homework already to make the marriage work. He mentioned a parent-daughter relationship, and if that didn't change, we were doomed for failure. What did he mean by that? My husband is bossy and controlling, isn't he? I'm the inferior one, am I not? OMG, I'm questioning my thoughts. *"That was a good thing,"* I said to myself. He gave us some techniques to work out. Leo's work paid the counselor we went to, that has to tell you something. *This guy's a quack.* I later found out he was on his third marriage.

Maybe he should take his advice quite while he's ahead.

I do think professional help is essential. Life is a roller coaster ride, and we all go through our ups and downs. A third party is always a good idea. My marriage was already an emotional roller coaster, and we were only in year two. Maybe I need to give it more time. I had overstayed my welcome at my girlfriends, so, what do I do?

I go back.

19

CHAPTER NINETEEN:

Tail Between My Legs

"Well, I'm back, house. Did you miss me?"

Why rock the family boat for my happiness? I did love him. Why would I have married him? I'm back, and I'm going to give it my all. The counselor said we had a child-parent relationship, so I decided to step up my game. I threw away soother and was ready to roll. I thought I was already grown up, but I decided to do better. I wasn't prepared for that type of relationship. The priest never talked about our feelings towards each. That would have been an excellent question to ask. "So what brings you here today? Why are you marrying each other? Do you love each other dearly or can you take it or leave it, the relationship? I prefer this question; If a train was coming down the tracks, and you could only save one person, would it be your boyfriend or your best, closest, dearest, girlfriend? Easy answer when it's not your soulmate, your girlfriend, of course.

And the marriage counselor told my hubby to take a chill pill. Have some fun, live in the moment, don't sweat the small stuff. He also asked him what was his obsession with the house, why it was so necessary to have the house paid off so quickly.

You shouldn't make your marriage all about money, but that's what he did without knowing it. I grew to hate that house when I should have loved it. It was a beautiful heritage house on a piece of property that drifted down the hill to the waterside. He did build an oasis for us.

When I stopped to breathe, I would look around and think that maybe I was just ungrateful. I was young, and 00perhaps I had to go back and put my head down and work harder to be the person he wanted me to be. I tried to do that.

I made myself busier than ever. I thought to myself, a*m I avoiding home, or just trying to keep working and make more money to keep up with the Jones?* I would train on the water in the mornings, head to my nine to five job, and then be back on the water or off to teach my fitness classes at a local school or church that I rented. We were always renovating the house. Thpaintbrush was my new appendage, and people were always pointing out I had a spot of paint on my skin somewhere.

I was a walking Benjamin Moore commercial. Besides the Renos, I had a great group of friends, and I was fortunate to be part of a fantastic staff at the office. I could let loose and vent to these people with my fun and games. I was pregnant with baby number two, when my long-time friend, a salesman, came into the office. He said I should apply for a position in their company in sales. I would have to travel a bit, but most nights I'd be home for the family. It was my opportunity to make some money.

I ran the idea by Leo, who immediately said no. "Your place is here with us with your family." Well he's right it is, but what an opportunity to bring home the bacon. He would have to do more around the house, like cook, laundry, and so on.

He made it sound like I was leaving on a mission to Mars. Maybe he was jealous because the opportunity came from a man, a male friend of mine. He accused me of having an affair with this man. I was eight months pregnant at the time. Honestly. The wall of bricks started to pile up on my shoulders. Its called resentment, and it will destroy a marriage.

Again I should have spoken up, but I let him win every time. I was exhausted.

Couples need to learn to argue early in their marriage, to learn to agree to disagree. We never did that. I'd always cave in or avoid the subject. One night my girlfriend called to go for a walk. "Sure," I said. I could use some fresh air. My husband always had to put in his two cents. He looked at me and said, "I thought we were going to walk together." He'd say it to serve up another dish of guilt. I replied, "You don't walk, you saunter; this is my exercise for today." I had to call her back. "Sorry, he wants to walk with me tonight." I can understand that once in a while, but he took any opportunity to take me away from my girlfriends.

I had no attachment to that house after I came back. I tried to make it my own, but I knew in my heart that he was married to the house, not to me. It was never going to be mine. Maybe it was ours in his mind, our painting, but I knew that he'd never leave. There was a thread of clam in the house. It felt like something was ready to erupt, but what? It was like an unspoken truth hovering over our house like a dark cloud. If there comes a time for one of us to leave, I know it will be me. He's made that very clear, like I'm on borrowed time there. *Be on your best behavior Emily*, I thought to myself.

20

Chapter Twenty:

Precious

*T*ime went on, and our friends were getting pregnant. I guessed it was time for the next phase of this marriage: children. Maybe that would bring us closer together. Leo knew that if I were ever to have children, I would want to adopt the first one.

I wasn't interested in my own. I wanted to adopt a child who was a lost soul and needed a loving family. My husband was adopted, and instead of paying it forward, he wanted his own. I agreed to his plan. *Of course, I caved. It's all about you, darling,* I thought to myself. We would have one of our own and then adopt one.

Getting pregnant was easy for me. We decided in July, and I was pregnant in August. Call me Fertile Myrtle. If I sat on the wet spot after sex, I'd get pregnant. Those little swimmers could smell their way to my egg.

Our first came nine months after summer rowing ended. What an experience! I loved being pregnant. The nausea passed after the first trimester. I continued working, training daily, and pretty well everything but drinking alcohol. It was a blast. I thought to myself, and *this gig is pretty straightforward.* Then the gynecologist suggested Lamaze classes since it was my first. I did the classes and gave in to my watermelon and green pepper craving. I gained sufficient weight, and the baby was expected around my birthday (but was overdue). Overdue?

I'm going to burst open at the belly. How can this child be happy all cocooned in there?

The doctor scheduled an induction. I was so ready to do this thing. That last month for women is crazy. It feels like you ate the entire watermelon and it just keeps rolling around in your body, putting pressure on your bladder, while the baby takes hip-hip classes, kicking anything they can reach. The best to describe the feeling of the baby's elbow grazing your tummy is by taking your tongue and rolling it around the inside of your cheek. You get heartburn with every meal, you pee your pants without sneezing, your breasts hurt and they start to drip colostrum, getting prepared for the milking factory you are going become. It's incredible and crazy at the same time.

There's no room at the Inn, the pressure is unreal, and you can't get comfortable. There's a tightening in your stomach and feels like that Alien baby is going to explode from your belly-button. It feels like you have to take a crap all the time. Anyway, that's a story for baby number two. Why didn't the Lamaze teacher fill me in on what induction was?

The Induction

If your doctor suggests induction for labor, don't be a hero, TAKE THE DRUGS! I told the doctor that I didn't want any drugs for pain, and for sure I didn't want an epidural. I want to feel the birth, What an idiot. They started a drip of a medication that would bring on the contractions. I had some time, so I put on my headphones and played some girl power Madonna tunes on my Sony player. An hour or so later, the contraction meds started kicking in. Holy shit, the contractions soon became stronger and closer together. The nurse came in to check to see how dilated I was. Two centimeters, that's it? I thought it would be a cakewalk, as I was in such great shape. I trained hard and could row through any type of lactic acid in my body, but nothing prepared me for these contractions. They were period cramps time one thousand.

Where was my husband? Coaching, of course. I asked the nurse if I could get up. She agreed, so I grabbed my drip and started pacing like a zombie in the hallway, looking for relief. I would have to stop frequently and breathe through it.

They rolled a screaming woman by me. She sounded like they were cutting her leg off or they were pulling her fingernails out. Either way, I didn't want any of that. A nurse came to check on me in the hallway. I asked her if that woman was going to be okay, and she said, "Yeah, they're just rolling her into the labor and delivery room. She's in labor." Was I going to get like that? What did I signup for? I decided I was only going to give this man one child!

The nurse came in again to check my dilation. I was only three centimeters, so I asked how far I needed to be. Didn't I listen to my Lamaze coach? She said nine centimeters, and that it was time for gas. Not the flatulence kind, either. It was supposed to help, but it just gave me the shakes.

Leo showed up just after the student doctor, *Doogie Howser*, saw me, the real doctor came back and had a good look at my crotch and said it was time. Leo looked at the nurse and suggested we close the curtains, as the window washer outside my window, was starring at my delivery.

By then I couldn't give a shit. If he wanted to crawl in the window and remove this kid, so be it. The doctor put his gloves on and got down low like he was catching for the Blue Jays. He poked his head around my leg and said to bear down. What I didn't know was that I didn't have enough room for the baby's head, so he was going to give me a small episiotomy so the baby could slide out nicely. Instead, I pushed hard on the beardown and ripped right open. The baby came slip-sliding out. She looked like she was covered in cottage cheese—that's another thing they don't tell you in Lamaze class. They had to suction her mouth and nose. Did you know babies are born with nose plugs?

She was a beautiful baby girl, healthy and eyes wide to the world. But my body wasn't done. I had to do another delivery—the placenta. The doctor then asked if I was allergic to any medications, and I said no. He gave me a needle to freeze my va-jay-jay and proceeded to stitch me up. My crotch must have looked like a roadmap, plus I was allergic to the local anesthetic. My lower lips swelled to the size of two avocados. I was a freak show for all the nurses. They were impressed: I had the most prominent set of lips in town without using a filler!

They put my Alix in my room, wrapped up in a little blanket in the incubator. She just lay there on her side, staring at me. I'm sure she was Cooing like a baby bird. Her eyes were big and brown. Nurses would come and go, looking at my crotch periodically but impressed at how fast my uterus was going down and that my young six-pack abs were still there.

Alix went from calm to hysterical in seconds. What does she want? Nobody was coming. OMG I'm her mother, I'm supposed to know. Blink once for food, two for a pooh! What am I saying, Emily get your child and figure it out? My sexy hospital gown was hanging off my shoulder for all to see. My crotch was killing me, I hobbled over to her, and picked the little bundle up. I will put her on my boob. Well by golly, she started breastfeeding right then and there. The human instinct is so beautiful. I started dripping from the other breast. Now, what do I do? The next morning, a random doctor came into my room. He didn't even look at me; he just stood in front of my bed and said, "You're being discharged this afternoon. If you have any complications, you can see me in my office." Then he walked out. *First of all, I gave birth last night and have twenty-five stitches in my va-jay-jay. I think I'm booked for a three day, all-expenses-paid vacation on the maternity deck. Plus, I need someone to show me how to bathe the baby. But if you want me gone, I'm gone.*

Leo walked in, and I was a bit upset. I told him he'd have to go home and get the car seat because we had to take Alix home that afternoon. A nurse came in during our conversation and saw me up and getting dressed.

"Where do you think you're going? The nurse said. I'm setting up a Sitz bath for you?" A Sitz bath is where your crotch goes to soak after it rips apart and the pressure causes large hemorrhoids. Now if that's not an invitation to a great party, I don't know what is.

"Home," I said. "A doctor came in and said I could leave now, and that he'd see me in his office next week."

"Was it your doctor?"

"No," I replied.

"Back to bed. I will straighten this out."

He had the wrong patient. He didn't recognize me. How could he? They never look at faces, just crotches.

We brought her home five days later, once my roadmap healed, and my lower lips were average size. We put her on the coffee table in her car seat and sat across from her on the couch. Nobody spoke; we just stared at her. I was amazed at what we had created together. Leo made it very clear, he would only change diapers in the home, if I wasn't around, and not when we are out in public. He must have a problem with shit, who doesn't.

21

Chapter twenty-one:
Anyone can be a Mother

*G*oodness, you need a license for a dog, but anyone who has a uterus can have a child of their own. And if your single and find yourself on welfare, you can have as many as you like. We ay you to have them. And please those children will never see Montessori school or get to Harvard, but those women have that best of the best upgrades of phones, televisions, Nintendo games and more. What happened to this society? That is a frightening thought. You are maybe setting higher standards for these women. And if that doesn't work, birth control. The pill, IUD or better yet a chastity belt, with a tattoo that reads, DO NOT ENTER!

I had no experience with children whatsoever. Well, there was one time when I was thirteen and agreed to babysit for my sister, who'd made plans and asked me to take her regular Saturday night gig. Those little boys were a nightmare. They were homeschooled, and the entire house was a Montessori playground. The little devils had their schedules. As I was running down the hall chasing one poopy bum, the other small penis was up playing the piano. When the parents arrived home that night, Curly, Larry, and Moe were lying on their family room floor watching the television, and I was asleep on the sofa. That was the only time I had contact with children until I had my own unless I hit them with my bike.

A medium once told me that my oldest daughter had been my mother in another life. I believe that now. Years after that reading, I found a book under the lounge chair I was sitting on in Florida. I couldn't put it down.

It was written by, *Brian Weiss*, a psychotherapist. He wrote about one of his patient's past life regressions. Through him, she recalled her past traumas from centuries ago that plagued her in this life: *Many Lives, Many Masters*. That book changed my life and how I see things. I now believe a group of souls, travel through the centuries together, playing different roles each lifetime. How else do you explain the feeling that you've known someone forever when you meet them for the first time? Because you have. Anyway, back to my first baby, Alix.

She just stared me down. Alix had the most prominent brown eyes and beautiful red lips I'd ever seen, like my dad's mom. She didn't look like either of us. Maybe the mailman. Kidding. If Alix could speak, she would say, "Emily, you have no clue what you're doing, do you? I'll take it from here." And she did.

I ran into Samarah, my long-lost friend after I had the girls. She said, "You've got kids?"

"Yes, three."

"Oh my god, you haven't killed them yet, or left them somewhere?"

I was amazed, as well. Maybe I was a mother in another life. Thank goodness. It all came so naturally. I felt like I was a kid myself. I could relate to the girls. I could also start my canvas, create my life with my girls on it.

We make all our mistakes with our first. Sterilize anything that falls on the floor, no five-second rule for your first kid. They might get germs. Don't leave them alone, on the changing table, floor, bed, they might roll-off. Honestly, they are a week old, and they're not going anywhere.

We make our mistakes with our first-born. Now if I could have given her to a family of ten for the first three years, she would have been well adjusted and not so spoiled. The first kid is like your first pancake: burnt on one side, soggy on the other. The rest are perfect.

When I was a baby, my mom left me to play in my walker, the next thing she heard was me heading down two flights of stairs into the basement, when she arrived to see me, in hysterics, I was upright, not a bruise, zipping around the cement basement floor.

Being a mother is what kept me going. Children can divert your attention from the real issues. It was three and a half years later before number two came along. I had to be sure I wanted more and was staying with Leo. I looked around at those families with one child and decided I needed a larger family. This house required more people living in it. Alix should have a sibling. A sister would be awesome. I love having Lesley in my life. At this point, I knew adoption was out of the picture, his picture, anyway.

Leo wanted a boy. Not surprised. What man secretly wouldn't want an extra set of testicles to hang around with? It wasn't in the plan. I do believe his sperm needed a talking too. They never took swim lessons. That brings me back to the Grade Seven health class.

All sperm must always have their penetrating caps on. They must stop and ask for directions: Go east or go west on Fallopian Tube Way? Slow swimmers to the left; fast swimmers to the right,

first one to the egg wins the prize. I think that was my interpretation of what the teacher was saying.

We had another girl, Madison. She was a peanut. We named her after Leo's grandmother. I had the biggest smile; Leo was happy she was healthy, but she didn't have a penis. She was a much more natural birth. My second baby had a head the size of a baseball and petite shoulders. The doctor wasn't necessary for that one. I just sat up in bed and farted her out. The umbilical cord acted like a bungee as she shot straight out of my crotch onto my legs. At least we were in the hospital. The nurse was in the room, so she helped, and so did Leo. The doctor came in later to deliver the placenta and to collect his paycheque.

That little one cried for six months straight. Madison was happy only with myself I'm guessing any baby who shot out of their mothers' va-jay-jay like a cannon-ball would have some separation problem. That took a lot out of me, as I still had Alix to contend with. But like any family, you get into a rhythm, and it all works out. The oldest was super jealous of her baby sister, as she was taking up all my time. Maybe Alix was supposed to be an only child.

One day I left Madison in her car seat, sleeping. The oldest, Alix, was on the sofa pretending to read a book. I was in the kitchen baking when I heard the baby scream. I ran in to find the oldest still on the sofa and a hysterical baby.

"Do you know why she's crying?" I asked.

Alix replied, "No."

I went back to the kitchen. It happened two more times. Finally, I was on to her. The last time I ran in, Alix was making it back to the sofa. I walked away but hid around the corner. This time I caught her in the act. She was poking the baby in the eyes. *Yikes! What a weird kid! Jealous?*

"Hey!" I said. "This is not appropriate behavior. If you do that once more, into the microwave, you go. Now don't go calling the Family and Child Services, " I would never stuff my kid into a microwave, don't worry. Well … I wouldn't close the door and turn it on.

A Christmas to remember 1994

We had just put a beautiful family room addition onto the house. Again, with the house. My sister and her family were coming from out west to spend Christmas with us. I was so excited. I loved having the whole family together for Christmas. I needed people around. They were my happiness, my constant. I tried to make our house a home. When it was full of people, it was good.

I can't speak for all mothers, but my mom would start discussing what we were eating for Christmas eve and day around Thanksgiving, right after the dessert. We love her, but honestly, when you are not a big foodie, the last thing you want to discuss is more food. It brought her a lot of joy and gave her something to plan. I'm guessing it's the same shit we ate last year and the previous 45 years; turkey, potatoes, ham, veggies and way too many desserts. Are we turning into that, our mothers?

Lesley and her family showed up for ten days. The kids played in the snow with their uncle, we baked our traditional Christmas cookies, and it was a great time. Leo's parents were always included. He had a distant sister whom we didn't see much. That Christmas was so much fun. It was great having all of us together throughout the holidays. I didn't realize how important family was until we were all together.

Leo and I were having our issues, as usual. We got through the Reno just before Christmas. That alone could cause a couple to divorce. Honestly, our entire marriage up to that point involved renovating. I put our differences on the back burner to enjoy my sister's family. There were a few nights I had a little bit too much to drink during their visit.

It wasn't until February that my girlfriend figured out that I was pregnant with number three. He said he'd pulled out! But I think he truly wanted to try for that boy. I was shocked at first, but I had to listen to the universe. It was telling me something. I had to have this baby. Most number threes are surprises for couples. I had a boy's name picked out from the beginning. His slow swimming sperm had no clue where they were going; the girls swam faster, and women always ask for directions. Of course, they find their way to the egg first. And along came Elizabeth.

Vasectomy, for a male, is the end of reproduction for them. It takes the choice away from a man, and the decision to have any more children in that life is made for him. All wrapped up into this one little procedure. It's a snip and concertizing to prevent those swimmers from getting the testicles. It sounds trivial to women who have barred children when you think of what we go through to have those babies — body change, hormone change, and then the birth.

I felt I did my part, and I made it very clear I wanted no more kids. I don't think Leo was happy with this decision. I remember him saying, "what if something happens to this baby? I replied, Then we have two beautiful daughters". He made the appointment while I was still pregnant with number three. But he selfishly canceled it. I made him call and booked it again. I finally said, "This is the last time. If you cancel again, I'll do it myself! It's amazing what you can find on the internet." It gave me much pleasure to see him lying on the sofa with a bag of frozen peas between his legs. I think back, and because of our instability, maybe he wanted to save his swimmers for another woman — another marriage. I don't know, we never discussed it. Again was I the selfish one? It has to be a joint decision.

Another Fight!

When Leo and I were out, we were a pretty good couple. We liked to go out with friends. One night we were driving home from a typical evening out. It was wet and slushy on the roads, and Leo was giving me his cold shoulder. In those cases, I'd get into the car and count to three. By one, he was on me. "I saw that guy looking at you. I saw you looking at that guy." Blah, blah, blah! It was always the same story and always my fault like I provoked it. Wy didn't I say something?

By the time I got to "one" in my head, he was asking twenty questions, as though he'd been watching me the entire night. Weird. He was so insecure. Maybe I made him that way. Well, on this night I'd had enough. I told him to pull over because I was getting out of the car.

"No," he said, "we are going home."

"Pull this fucking car over; I'm getting out." And I did just that. While the car was still in motion, I opened the door and put my foot on the road. I was spraying icy slush everywhere. He finally stopped the car, as he knew that I meant business. "Your jealousy is killing this marriage," I said. Why don't you trust anyone? You act like we are all going to leave you, we are not!"

I didn't have it in me to fight. How did we create this pattern?

Was I at fault for not communicating to him, standing up for myself? Maybe. He was becoming very suspicious, probably because I was becoming very distant with him and with life.

Leo and I have very different personalities, and maybe our needs were different. Again we lacked communication so were drawn from our own conclusions about the other person. Absurd.

22

CHAPTER TWENTY-TWO:

Parenting 101

*C*hildren are easily influenced at such a young age. They're human sponges, absorbing life's observations into their pores. They observe the world day and night. They watch their parents and imitate their behavior.

Did I need Dr. Spock telling me how to nurture these little creatures I ejected from my loins,

Hell No! One day I was in the car with my three daughters, aged eight, five, and three. Alix, the oldest, started on her big sister's speech: "Now girls, there are five words we should never repeat: damn, hell, shit, bitch, and fuck." I looked at my daughter, so proud. She said, "Right, Mommy?" I thought to myself, *These sad little humans, do they know who their Mother is?* Time to get out the swear jar.

I adored my little people. That's what I called them. I love being their mother; it's truly the most rewarding job you can have. The rewards don't happen until they get a little bit older. You get to go through a rediscovery of the world with them when they're little people and then become their friend as they get older. We all lived by the calendar: What's going on before school? After school? Before dinner? After dinner? Someone always had a commitment we had to get to. Schedules and more schedules, month by month until another year goes by and you can't recall the last. Another birthday, another Easter and Christmas, followed by Happy New Year. What year are we ringing in?

If I knew then what I had known now, I would have slowed us down to a crawl. Less of everything. More of nothing. More downtime.

As a parent, the days turn into weeks, months, and years. Before you know it, they're off to university or traveling the world, as my girls did. You're left to rediscover your own life as an empty nester. Now, look at that man sitting across from you. Is he the man you can't wait to travel, play golf with, or sit on a beach and read with? Or do you look at that stranger and say, "Holy shit, who is that man across from me? Who am I? I don't even like us". I'm not going to let us get to that point in our marriage. I will keep working on it. I feel most women in my position keep plugging away because we put everyone first, so our feelings aren't as important at the time. They can wait. Happiness is on hold, meaning we experience emotional loneliness. I tried to keep up with our Saturday night date night. I told Leo if we don't do something for ourselves, we will lose us.

And the trophy goes too!

I knew our marriage was going to be a competition. I felt inferior to Leo, not his equal. He always had me against the ropes, mentally. I was still questioning my parenting skills. He made me feel unworthy of the position. I was the lax parent, and he laid down the law. It was a good fit. We didn't play good cop, bad cop. Or wait till your father gets home parenting. I just felt he didn't take me seriously. Or because of my laid-back attitude, he thought he had to carry the weight.

I was younger, not by much in a parenting standard. Did I lack proper parental skills? Maybe he was too serious, and I not severe enough. If he wanted to pick up a second job, I would stay home and raise my children properly. That wasn't an option, so I stepped up my game.

I was a good mother. He was a good loving father. Too good, too smothering. Could I have been better if my head were in a better place emotionally? How many women feel that way? I look back and see that I had two options: stay or go. I waited instead of rocking the boat. He would have badgered me to death had I left with the kids. He threatened to get his lawyer involved and take full custody, claim I wasn't a fit mother. If I did leave, it wasn't going to be with my children. He would belittle me first and bring in the lawyers, so I stayed and played the game. That man had many badges on his Boy Scout sash. Do boy scouts have sashes? Well, his super cape then. If I could I would stitch them on myself and bedazzle the edging so it would sparkle day and night, he could wear it to the parent-teacher interviews, coaching or just out to the Canadian Tire so everyone would know he's a star father.

Was it guilt, blackmail or maybe I made him feel just insecure? As I've said, we were competitive people at heart, at least in sports. I never wanted us to compete in parenting. I just wanted him to pull his weight. That's an argument for most couples. I agreed with most of his parenting decisions, but he thought the worst possible outcome at times, so it was always a battle. We didn't realize it until we parted ways. We saw things differently from the beginning. That should have been my first clue. I decided that I was a successful person in all my endeavors, and I would make this marriage work one way or another. In my kids' eyes, I was emotionally stable, but I think there were times when my ghost took over. Have you ever heard the saying, "Fake it 'til you make it"? I'm very good at that. A robotic shell of me would raise the family. I was angry that I, the person I am now, couldn't come out to play. I should have been that happy, loving mother in that house with the kids. I was, but I feel I denied them the experience of two people romantically in love and parenting as a team. I was not a good role model for them.

I was always with my kids but mentally trying to escape the sadness. They told me once, "Mom, you should have left years ago when we were younger. It would have been easier for us." He would never have let me walk away without a significant fight, a custody battle, and more. Who wants that? I didn't. And where do you go with three little people and no home? Can I put them in a low-income apartment, after living in a substantial Victorian home?

Time passed, and I felt there was no way out, so I lived by the priest's words: 'Til death do you part". Does that mean if one partner dies during the marriage, the other one is free of the weight? That the bricks would leave my shoulders? I think so.

No one should have to live like I did—a life in which you have to pull away from your family home and to work to feel all that weight leave you. At work, I'd allow myself to be free for eight hours. I'd go into my happy place. There I got to be that other person, the one that everyone wants to be twenty-four hours a day—sunny, spontaneously funny me. Instead, I settled for eight hours of emotional freedom.

Then it would be time to go home, and as I got closer; my chest would get heavy. As I'd pull into the driveway, the bricks would be back on my shoulders. By the time I'd open the front door and walk in, that other person, the person I hated, would show up. I hated myself for years for being so weak. Maybe it was a sacrifice I was willing to make.

I was down at the rowing club one morning for my morning paddle. I was friends with Leo's first lawyer. He was always handing out legal advice. He told me years later that he gave my ex some legal advice after I left the first time. He told him to buy me out with a small amount. "She's young and has no idea what the house is worth," he'd said.

I never took the deal, as he never had the chance to offer it to me. I returned to Leo and vowed to stick it out. He was like my big, bossy brother. How can you have any romantic thoughts about your brother? Leo and I had painted two different pictures for ourselves. He loved being the man of the house and in control of all the big decisions. He also had to be part of everything I did outside of work.

Was he jealous of my happy-go-lucky personality, or that I had family roots? I knew my family's history, and where I came from, he did not. I had a variety of friendships and was always getting invited out. I couldn't just clear my schedule and go out; I had to ask permission to do anything. He had control over me. It was so robotic. Whether it was just a dinner out or a girls' weekend away, it was unheard of. He'd cry, "We never get to go out. We need a weekend away." *No, Leo. I do, you idiot and so do you!* If only he treated me as his equal, I would have done the same. I would push him out the door if he were invited out of town for a hockey tournament. We would have had a stronger marriage if he trusted me. He laid on the guilt thick like he was buttering bread — smooth move. You gain trust when you give it.

"Okay, I will stay home," I'd say out loud. Then under my breath, I'd mutter, "I hate you, why do you play this game with me?."

Vulnerability is scary

OMG! I love your home and the backyard. It is so amazing here like a cottage setting. Must you enjoy being on the water? I was told that always. My reply would be," Thanks, Have you ever tried to take care of a home this size, I need a goat to eat the weeds on the bank, and a weekly cleaning lady to keep up inside. It's a make-work project.

So the answer is, No, I don't love living here. Why should I, when what I see is twenty-four-seven upkeep. I tried to decorate and enjoy the backyard when there was time, but I never gave in to enjoying my home, his home, the way I should have. I was always a bit detached from it and him. I think I always knew I would be leaving it, the house I spent over half of my life growing up in, and maybe he did too. And when that day comes, I don't want to feel that sadness, that hurt, that lose of attachment, so I bury those enjoyable moments, and swallow those emotions. I feel nothing when I leave. How empty was that?

It's like never getting a dog because you know one day it will die, and that will make you feel awful. We do this to ourselves. We don't want to be disappointed, so we don't set our selves up for it. There's that old saying, " Never expect anything, and you will never be disappointed." And if something significant happens, that brings us happiness, and we wait for the ball to drop. We play out the worst-case scenario in our heads. We have prepared ourselves for the worst. Why?

If I just gave into that fear and honestly loved that home, maybe I could have loved Leo more. I don't know.

Recurring Dream

Bloody hell, I'm still waking in a sweat from this stupid dream. I'm lying under a wall of rubble with the person standing over me. I was up above, watching everything. I couldn't understand why I couldn't move. Maybe that was my subconscious mind telling me something. I knew I was being smothered in my marriage. I was starting to suffocate in my own body, but I never showed it. Or was I? I surrounded myself with outlets. The bricks I talk about, the ones that weigh me down every day when I arrive home, are they the same ones that cover my bloody body?

I've had this dream once a month for forever it seems. I looked it up. Dream experts say,

They say that many people have the same or a similar dream many times, over either a short period or their lifetime. Recurring dreams usually mean there's something in your life, causing stress that you've not acknowledged. The dream repeats because you haven't corrected the problem. I'm working on a solution. It may take time.

A Parent's Valuable Lesson

As we all know, parenting is bloody exhausting. You can only do that tour once. Parents who have one child and say they're busy is like saying you're full after the appetizer. That's not the whole meal! I call parents with two kids, one boy and one girl, the token family. You are complete. One child for each parent. Two kids, sitting comfortably in the backseat, with enough space in between to break up the fights.

North American evolves around the perfect four. It's a world built on families of four. The kitchen tables have four seats, our vehicles four comfortably. Two parents, two children. When you throw in a third child, it throws your world off-balance. But I wouldn't change a thing. Our children are gifts from above. They're here to teach us something, and they learn from us along the way—the good stuff and the bad.

With the third child, I felt forced to put my game face on. Get organized and, Ugh, buy a Minivan. We had to run a tight ship. We had schedules to keep, lunches to make, activities to get to, and deadlines to meet. There were days when you were spinning out of control.

And don't let those perfect Moms fool you at school, I'm sure they left a child or too behind when they were in a rush. Well I did. Yes, Elizabeth was bundled up in her car seat on the kitchen table ready to roll. It wasn't until Alix said, "Mommy wheres Elizabeth?" Madison replied in her two and a half-year-old voice, " table." "What!" I replied. I turned around and began to panic. Back we go. I hope I didn't leave her in the driveway, Oh shit, or onto of the car. No, no, you don't put babies onto of cars just coffees. I pulled into the driveway, no baby, ran back into the house to find her sweating profusely in her snowsuit, on the table.

I Envied stay-home moms. It made parenting a piece of cake. You are honestly home all day or at the school, driving the teachers crazy. You might find yourself at the gym, or yoga and lunch dates with your other stay-home moms. Is this punishment? I thought parenting was going to be fun. I just wanted to play with my girls, and enjoy their company. Screw the piano lessons, activities, and soccer practices. Too much discipline. Why do we put so much pressure on all of us? It can all be too much. I remember asking Leo if we could forfeit soccer for summer and spend more time at the cottage or visit our friends in P.E.I. We never got there. "The girls can't miss soccer!" Leo would say. I wonder if he regrets that decision.

I remember sitting outside in the car, waiting for Elizabeth, my youngest daughter. She toogymnastics a couple of times a week. She wasn't coming out, so I went inside to get her. She was sitting on the bench, crying. I asked her what was wrong, and she said, "The coach is so mean. I don't want to go back in."

At first, I was stunned. She'd been going to this club for a few years, ten hours a week. I was going to convince her to stay, but I didn't. *Snap out of it, Emily*, I thought to myself. I was ridiculous. I knew she wasn't going to be another Mary Lou Retton. She was good, but it wasn't about her talent; it was about her enjoyment. She wasn't enjoying it anymore. These are situations where you don't have to finish out the year, and there was no recital they were practicing.

I said, "Sit tight, kid, I'll be right back."

I ran back into the club and explained to the coach that her approach was too harsh for Elizabeth, and she wouldn't be returning. I then jumped back into the car.

"Lets' go home for ice cream," I said. "You don't have to go back. Ever." She looked at me with the utmost respect and gave me the biggest hug and kiss. I learned a valuable lesson that day. We push our kids, but why? Do we as parents feel that if our children, as adults start something then than they automatically won't finish? "That's Malarkey," as Lucy would say. Of course, they will, if they enjoy it. I spent thousands on piano lessons. Why?

I needed to start looking at life through my children's eyes, not mine. Leo as well.

Rice or chili

Besides the runny noses, diarrhea in the diapers, there's puke — nobodies friend. And you better not have a weak stomach for this gig. It's usually everywhere. As a parent, we dread the day when our puke feast happens. When your single and you find yourself throwing up, someone is generally holding your hair because you had one too many tequila shots. I wasn't sick often as a kid maybe twice, always on a school playday of course. The one time, I stood in my parent's bedroom, to inform them I had a tummy ache. Before I knew it, chili was hurling out of mouth like The Exorcist. Those were the days of shag carpeting. My parent's carpet was orange in color. They were racking up kidney beans and pieces of onion for months. So when I'm offered chili, I have a flashback, then say no thank-you. For our daughters it was rice, but we didn't know who puked on who. The girls slept with each other at night. I never knew where anyone was until the morning. There was a sour smell coming from Alix's room. When I went in, it looked like a Chinese massacre. White rice everywhere. They all had long hair. When its called, sticky rice, it's sticky. They were covered it. The girls slept through someone sitting up puking on her sisters, rolling over and going back to bed.

My husband was a great provider. We had a beautiful country home on the water, with a beautiful. We were situated on a waterway, so living there was like living at a cottage. We were keeping up with the Jones. I think we ran our home like most people. We did the best we could with what we had at our disposal. We were a middle-income couple with three kids to raise. I remember saying a few times, "I think this place is too expensive to live in, and the property taxes are crazy. If we downsized, we'd have more disposable income." Leo would say nothing.

I even tried to get him to do a house exchange in Australia. He'd work there, and we'd live in their home, and they would do the same at our place. "Nope. Australia is your dream, not mine," he'd say. Okay, fine. I decided to keep that on the back burner.

My favorite part of the day was dinner time. We'd go around the table and ask, "What was your high and what was your low today?" For me, it was all about experiences in life. I loved hearing about my kids' day. It brightened up mine. I'd often have a funny story to tell about a patient or my boss. We tried so hard to keep up with this façade. The portrait of our perfect little family. We even had the white picket fence.

Why do we feel the need to showcase our success in the car we drive or the house we live in or the cottage we own? It's not a competition—or is it? Did the schools ruin us from day one? Did we have to give every kid a participation ribbon for play day or track and field? Who cared how many sit-ups or push-ups Bobby Bobak could do for his Award of Excellence badge? We did! Our cars and homes are just more prominent badges and trophies for some of us. Status symbols. I hated the Jones. I'm not interested in keeping up with anybody. I wanted to live within our means, without any pressure.

23

CHAPTER TWENTY-THREE:

Painting a Picture-
The hats to prove it

J wore a lot of hats in that house. Most women do. I just thought Leo could do more on his days off. One day I left him a note on my way to work: "Please pick up their school uniforms." When I returned home after work, I found that note ripped up. Later, he commented, "Emily, you have your jobs to do, and I have mine. If you can't fulfill yours, just let me know." Who was he talking to, one of his trainees? Until I left, I don't think he understood how much I did.

"Wow, that's harsh," I replied. No one deserves that put down. I stopped asking and just did my thing, but a hot ember of resentment was fueling the fire inside of me. He ran the house like he was at work. I always told him to keep his business there — another red flag.

Why was this a big deal for me? I felt he wasn't pulling his weight, but when I spoke up, he'd go on the defensive and throw a punch of guilt right down my throat. I was young, but for the most part, I thought couples fell into a rhythm together. They see where their assets lie and where they're most needed.

Leo had the outdoor chores, and I had the rest. He divided the duties up into seasons. With Leo's work, he had days off in a row to get stuff done around the house. But I couldn't ask him to do more—than would be like confessing that I wasn't capable. I put so much pressure on myself to be what he wanted to keep the peace. But inside I was a volcano ready to erupt.

What is the real role of women here on earth? Why do we so much pressure on ourselves to do everything, and do it well. Who are we trying to impress? Is it to be a successful professional, a leader in the workforce, as we all insist on gender equality? Is it just to get married? Have children? Or be the creation of God, to be the motivating engine and facilitator of life here on earth? Is it to find happiness and peace in yourself and others? They don't teach any of this in Home economics. I needed a life skills course in my twenties. What was Emily's role in Leo's house?

Role Model

After giving birth to three girls, I started asking myself these critical questions: What role was I playing? If I worked, was I showing them an active, independent professional? If I could multi-task, did that show organization? If I took care of the body and kept it in the proper physical condition and respected it than I was doing a good job. I became more aware of what I was doing and how Leo would speak to me. I was a role model for these young women. I needed to show him respect so they would.

I wish I knew then what I know now about the universe and how she operates. I have fantastic advice for my daughters, but they have their road to travel and their blank canvas to paint.

Women need to feel that they're contributing something more than children, into the marriage. I felt that financially when it comes to running a home, I needed it contribute more. I hated that feeling. Was it my insecurity? Did Leo make me feel wrong about my work? My mother and sister both had fantastic jobs in health care. Was I judging my self worth by my career choice? I loved my job.

Leo's choice of location, put pressure on our family to stay within a tight budget. We had to make those sacrifices to live there. Was it worth it in the end? Maybe that's why I hated living there, and it made me feel like I wasn't contributing enough. I honestly think at that time; if I suggested moving, he would have shown me the door. I wanted us to be happy and live simpler lives.

Would we still be married? Probably not.

I always appreciated what Leo brought to the table in this marriage, and I would go about my own business at the same time. Leo had some great qualities. He loved those girls, and he was an excellent coach. He coached every sport they took part in. Help but up the nets and gather up the balls, depending on the competition. There was always work involved for them. They appreciate it now. My girlfriend and I tried coaching soccer to six-year-olds one summer. I never played the game, and I never watched a game until my oldest started playing. I played ball and wanted the kids to give it a try, but Leo wasn't having any of that. But that summer, we learned team spirit, about every player has equal opportunity to play, and most importantly, how to do a proper cartwheel. After each goal scored, everyone was to do a cartwheel in celebration that I could do. We had a great summer, and all those kids came back the following year.

I still didn't feel like his equal, and he was still the parent to me. This was his landscape, not mine. I, in turn, felt like Quasimodo, busy ringing the bell all day long until the boss came home. We were a good team, we ran a tight ship, without the OCD kicking in. I think we mastered that well. We were a bit unbalanced, but that was the way it was.

The cleaning Lady

I cleaned our house daily but working out of the house with three kids and a hairy dog, I thought I would give a cleaning lady a try. It was coming out of my pocket, so I went through a few with the white glove test. One day I took ill and came home early. Isobella was at our place cleaning. I pulled in the driveway and heard music coming from inside. I snuck around to find my cleaning lady was hitting those piano keys like there was no tomorrow. I wasn't paying her to serenade the dog, and I was paying her to suck up his dog hair.

I tapped her on the shoulder and said, "thank you for coming." She replied in her best English/Spanish accent, "Chour piano keys are zo dirty, I chas cleening chem." I paid her and gave her the boot. I can do this job myself. I was wasting an entire evening cleaning up before she came anyways. Screw it!

Then I thought to myself, *well at least someone is playing that piano after all those lessons.*

The War of the Roses

Do you remember the 1989 movie, *The War of the Roses*, with Kathleen Turner and Michael Doulas? Up until their last breath, they wouldn't cave, show their emotions, make-up, and forgive each other. Sometimes you need to cut your losses and run. No hard feelings. Or wait until a chandelier falls on your head.

I can see how individuals can keep themselves so busy that they don't have to face reality. They create another reality that blocks the part that hurts. Then the financial burden sets in. It did for me, anyway. He was determined to pay off our mortgage at all costs. I wanted to give us more, give our daughters more, but I wasn't the primary breadwinner, just his slave. Here's an example for you: We'd had an old mattress since we were first married, and we needed a new one. He had a bad back, so it was time.

"No," he said, "this one is fine. If you want another mattress, you go buy one". He knew I couldn't afford it. You are just shaming me to a point where I didn't feel worthy.

Really? What the fuck? Now that's a one-sided marriage. I should have gone out and purchased one, but we didn't share a bank account or a credit card. I couldn't afford one on my salary. I wanted one shared bank account, but something stopped me in my tracks. If he hawkeyed me about spending, then I would have to stay on my toes, always. I didn't want him questioning my credit card purchases constantly. I didn't need that shit, that's for sure. Lesson learned, honey.

There was a time when I asked for a new bedroom set for our first daughter, and he said no.

I would go to yard sales and buy used furniture and refinish it. I made each one of their rooms special. I realized they didn't require a brand- a new set, but we had the money, and he liked to control it.

My marriage was full of lessons, even after I left him. Red flag!

We all know that running a household and organizing a family is a full-time job if you're doing it correctly. Throw in a career, and you might as well forfeit your sanity, especially when the household tasks are not shared. Grocery shopping and laundry were endless. Breadwinner or no breadwinner, it doesn't matter who brings home the bacon or who makes the most. That's a crock of shit. Everything in and out of the house should be done fifty-fifty to keep the couple married and sane. One cooks, the other cleans up, and vice versa. I believe different strokes for different folks, whatever works, but in my experience, for a couple to appreciate one another equally, the tasks should be spread out reasonably as well.

I was saturated with cleaning the house, grocery shopping, cooking every meal, doing all the laundry and folding, and other tasks around the house like painting and refinishing. There would be days when he was off, I would walk in the door, and four of them would be sitting at the kitchen table wondering what we were having for supper. Really? Hit me with another brick, please!

Most nights if he was home and the kids had a game, he would make his famous pasta meal, which was cooked noodles with butter and maybe some parmesan cheese sprinkled on it. By the time I got home, my pasta dinner was the leftover noodles stuck in the colander in the shape of a bowl. He could have at least tried, opened a cookbook, or taken some lessons. He never made an effort to improve. He put that on me. It was so old fashioned like it was my job because I had breasts. That bothered me. He was BBQing one time while reading the newspaper, and he burnt the chicken. One of the girls commented that it would be the last time he BBQed if anyone said anything ever again. Wow, Mr. Sensitive. Stubborn! We, the girls, loved the kitchen. Alix was an excellent cook, and we all enjoyed baking. It was my meditation. Maybe Leo felt outnumbered.

24

CHAPTER TWENTY-FOUR:

Queen of Laundry

*H*umans started wearing clothes to cover up their hairless bodies, 170,000 years ago. When did we realize these garments required laundering? Who knows, but someone had to wash them, hang them, and fold them. It was the women's job, and she stayed home to keep the fire burning, cook over it, and yes, laundry. It was and still is the number one full-time, unpaid job. If you love doing laundry, you need to get a life. I had a girlfriend who ironed their pillowcases. I have been in a cave all my life.

If you both work, you both do laundry. When did our society decide that we required more than one outfit of everything? One outfit for work, play, school, and church. The scrubboard has been around since 1797 until someone formed a band and they decided it made a better instrument then stain remover. A wonderful man by the name of James King invented and patented the actual washing machine in 1851.

Well, in my homes, this was my job, and it was a full-time gig. I did laundry almost every day but Sunday. I saved the mystery sock basket for Sundays. Occasionally, I'd find a matching pair of socks from it, and I'd be elated. You must celebrate the little pleasures in life. One day when I was having a pity party for myself I tossed all these unmatched socks into the garbage. I thought I was going to lose my shit, like an alcoholic pouring his Booze down the drain. I couldn't stand it, I went back to the garbage and retrieved the socks. There are people on the street with cold feet, and I'm throwing mismatches socks like money grows on trees. That's for you, Lucy!

In all my years, I never saw Leo fold anything, not one stitch of clothes. Maybe he was a closet folder and didn't tell me.

I did see him use one of those twisted wire things before, the ones you break into cars with.

Yes, they are hangers. Let's have some assembly in this closet. I was starting to resent that man. I understand different strokes for different folks. Some couples share all the duties or divide them up. But when you have a busy family always on the go, pick up the slack, man. I'm sure I asked, cringed a few times, with no outcome. So we would fall into our life's habits, resenting them, instead of yelling at them, and stuffing a sock in their mouth.

Once a week, I'd ask, "Are you ever going to help with the laundry?" He just sat there so complacent.

"Nope," he would reply.

Can I kill him now? Hell no, I'll get blood all over the bright whites!

I trained my little three monkeys to do their part. "If it's not in the basket, it doesn't get washed," I'd shout daily. "For God's sake, I leave your folded clothes on the stairs, so you'll take them to your room, but you just walk by them!" It seems that was all I did—laundry, laundry, laundry. With three little girls, it never stopped.

I remember one day he suggested we conserve energy and hang all our laundry outside to dry. He was going to put up a little clothesline. Holy shit that better be a considerable clothesline may be extending from one telephone pole to another. I just laughed out loud and replied, "Are you fucking serious? We have five people living here! I'm the only one who does the laundry in this house. Why not move the kitchen to the back yard so I can cook at the same time? How many hours in a day do I have?" Or better yet, get me a big old rock, and I will scrub the clothes against it.

"If you want to conserve water and energy, let's go pick out a brand-new set." That didn't happen. I took my girlfriend's mother's old set. Leo said they were in good working order. I'm sure I saw the same machines on the, *Leave it to Beaver Show*. I bet June Cleaver got new set when her old ones died.

We will squeeze another few years out of them. "*I will do the same with you,*" I said myself.

The fire is growing!

Grandparents-Can I keep them?

As I said in the beginning, I only remember having one grandparent, and she didn't take to me. Like flies to honey, I was more like the plague to her. When I met my husband's parents, I was elated. They were the most adorable couple I'd ever met. They were both retired and happier than a pig in shit together. His dad's name was Lenny. We had a great relationship, and he had a great relationship with my kids. He was a funny little European man. He was a typesetter for our newspaper so that he could spell anything. He always played games with the kids, like little spelling bees at the table, and he still had dirty jokes for us. He was always smiling. His middle name was Valentine, and he was, made of love. Lenny was a man who had a song for Diarrhea and many more. He was a vet in WWII and played the ukulele for the troops.

There are lots of funny stories about Lenny, but here are a couple.

He was a talented painter as well. His portfolio included quite a few sketches of nude women, and they were terrific. One day his wife said, "Lenny, can you not paint something else besides a nude woman? Like this hat?" The next picture he did was his wife's enormous straw beach hat. He said, "How do you like your hat?" She said," that perfect." A few days later t appeared in the living room with a beautiful nude woman sitting cross-legged, on the beach, under it.

On Remembrance Day, I dressed Lenny in his officer's jacket and medals. He would go to the kid's school and share his war stories with them once. He was telling the kids about how he and two other soldiers, had to hide on a pig farm, in the pig shit, during the day and wait for his boat to find them at night. One little girl raised her hand and asked Lenny if he knew her grandfather because he was in the army. He said,

"Why yes, I knew Bill Brown very well. Too bad he's dead." You should've seen this little girl's face. "How could Papa be dead?" she asked. "I just had supper with him on Sunday." OOPS!

My mother-in-law passed away first, and she said to me, " Don't put Lenny in a home when I'm gone, he will die there.", so then we moved my father-in-law into the house. Leo had built a beautiful in-law suite for him so he could live with us but also have some space for himself. He would still be with the family and eat with us as much as he wanted to. Did I mention Lenny was legally blind? He would find his way to the bus stop and away he went. He ventured across the busy street to bow with the blind bowers. Blind bowling? Why not blind lawn darts, were my thoughts. But when I went over to watch him, people assisted them with their balls. Ok, go check it out for yourself.

One day he took a spill in our house, and that started a downward spiral that led to his eventual death. I recall his final days. We moved him to a quiet hospital in Niagara-on-the-Lake, where he could die with dignity. Every day I would sit with him, place earphones over his ears, play his favorite music, and wait for Marsha, his deceased wife, to get him. Lenny couldn't wait to check out. He had a date with her and couldn't be late. They had front row seats to see his favorite performer, Pavarotti. The venue was the opening ceremony for the 2010 Olympics in Turin, Italy. He slowly drifted away, with all of us by his side. After his last breath, my brother-in-law, Lesley's husband, Napoleon, said a lovely heartfelt prayer. The nurse then moved the family from his bedside to a family room to rest.

She said, "the opening ceremonies for the winter games are commencing. I will turn them on for you."

He passed away fifteen minutes before Pavarotti hit the stage. He didn't stand her up, and he was just in time. *Enjoy the show old man*, I thought to myself. Always punctual.

Those were good times. Maybe I stayed with Leo because his parents gave me something I was missing in life—loving grandparents.

25

CHAPTER TWENTY-FIVE:

Bunions- curse or blessing

*W*hy do women punish their feet for looking good? Ws it heels or tight-fitting hockey skates or did t, grandpa have bunions? In this family, hereditary. I had so many problems with my feet. I had a hard time sleeping, running, walking, or doing anything for which I had to use footwear. Flip flops were my savior. My bunions were killing me. I found a doctor who suggested a bilateral reconstruction of my feet. He wanted to perform the surgery one foot at a time, but I suggested he do both. That way I'd be done. I heard it was a painful surgery, and if I were taking time off work, it would be better to do both at once. That's what he did in the summer of '99. OHIP bought me a pair of fiberglass casts and some time off work. Right after the surgery, they wheeled me into recovery, and my legs were covered with the sheet. I told the nurse who was wandering by that I needed to go to the bathroom. She said sure and kept walking. I swung my legs around and tried to stand, before I knew it, I was under the bed. Fiberglass is very slippery on a hospital floor. I must have made a noise, as she came running back in. She said, "I didn't know you had both feet done at the same time?"

I would have been stuck in upstairs for ten weeks unless I learned to slither off the bed, and crawl around on my bum or go backward in the walker. A loaner from my girlfriend, Patricia. It wasn't beneficial with a two-story home. I had to count on my husband to take care of the kids, do the laundry, and make the meals. I didn't care at this point; I was in pain; I had to go through with the surgery. The first night home, I was lying in bed, and he ran by me saying, "I'm taking the kids to soccer practice. We'll see you later." I was like, "I need some supper!"

He ran back upstairs and threw me a block of cheese, a knife, and a box of crackers, saying he'd be back in a few hours. I thought I was going to wither away if I had to rely on Leo for nourishment. I'm glad my mother and friends were around the corner. Only ten weeks of this. How will I ever stay put? I don't stop moving.

There were days when I was home, and everybody was gone, and I'd be on the kitchen floor, washing it. Have you ever tried vacuuming your home on your ass? It's challenging, indeed. I found a package of microwave popcorn, but then reality set in. The microwave was at eye level when standing. Bloody hell! It seemed miles away. I thought I was going to starve to death. The fridge was bare. They'd come home to find me back in bed like nothing happened that day. I was a princess eating bonbons watching my soaps. Nobody noticed the house was clean.

I had amazing friends, so one day I was very excited when I heard the knock at the back door. My friend said, "Where are you? I've got coffee and a muffin for you." Sweet Jesus, a human. "I'm up here," I cried. My girlfriend ran upstairs to find me on the bathroom floor. I slipped off the toilet. I forgot I was wearing fiberglass skates.

The surgery slowed me down, and I had no choice. My mom was a big help while I was healing. The kids were nine, six, and three at that time, so they required plenty of attention. They were also very self-sufficient, making their lunches, getting themselves dressed. My girlfriend, Patricia, would visit in the afternoon and we would have fancy umbrella drinks around the poolside with the little ones.

I could hear Robin Leach, from the TV show, *Lifestyles of the Rich and Famous*, in my backyard on Elm Street. "*Emily started as an average housewife, slaving for her useless husband, Leo, when, after one botched up foot-surgery, Emily could afford a lifestyle of luxury for herself and her friends.*" Now it's pool-sides, fancy drinks and a lifetime of wealthy shallow acquaintances. Ok, I was in my happy place; I would never put a paper umbrella in my glass.

I enjoyed the pampering. If I needed two casts on my feet to slow me down, then so be it. I had an excuse to sit. The universe was trying to tell me something. Again.

We all need to stop and smell the roses once in a while. We need to simplify our lives again. Live in the moment and be present always. Slow down and reflect. I'm speaking from experience, of course. During my time as a parent raising the girls, I was whirling around like the Tasmanian devil. Those ten weeks laid up in casts forced me to reflect on my life and ask myself some valuable questions: Where is this marriage going? Do I want someone else running my life for me? Do I want to raise three little girls on my own? Could I afford it?

Women face these questions every day when they're unsatisfied with their relationships. I started to journal more. I had to hide it under the mattress, as Leo was a shift worker. He was home often when we were all gone for the day. I introduced journaling to our children as a time to reflect and put down your thoughts, to clear your mind. It brings on sleep and empties the mind.

I don't think people journal as much anymore. Putting your day's experiences and feelings on paper is so healthy. My sister has done this ever since I can remember. Kudos to her. I must have journaled enough that I took all those thoughts and put them into this book. I journaled throughout my marriage, but towards the end, he would read it and write back in it. That's a red flag!

FOMO

I struggled with this during the last fifteen years with Leo. The fear of missing out, FOMO, is anxiety that an exciting or interesting event may currently be happening elsewhere. It's often aroused by posts on social media and can be very stressful for people. I had this as a kid in a small way. I hated to miss a party or an event at school, but I don't think it created a problem. There was no social media then. One Friday afternoon came around, and I had no clue what all my peeps were doing, except for my besties. Sure, you'd try to make a few plans before you left school, but all in all, the weekend would go by, and you'd let life play out. We'd make plans on a dime, do our own thing with family or friends on the street, or if you had a car, you'd hit a house party or two. That's about it. Monday would roll around, and you'd tell your friends about the weekend.

I believe our younger generation suffers from FOMO in a big way. With the click of a mouse or the tap of a screen, they know where their 1,785 friends are, what they're up to, what they're eating, and who is hanging with whom and where. People can share every moment of their lives. There are so many facades of social media, and I can't keep up. But I don't want to. Once you cleanse yourself from it, you don't miss it. You start living in the moment instead of capturing it to share with everyone. Yes, there are times I want to share a picture, a moment, or my thoughts, or connect with distant friends, but not daily. I don't think Facebook or Instagram should be an aid in helping inform your peeps what you're up to every minute of the day. The option to "like" or "block" creates a control in all of us. It also hurts people, plays on their emotions. I also think some people define their life by the number of followers they have on social media. Is life a popularity contest? On that note, if you are in sales or marketing your product its a fantastic platform.

The Ghost in the House

There was a woman in my dream from the seventeenth century. Let's call her Sarah. She told me what to do. Sarah painted a picture of a seventeenth-century dining room in my head. She was standing at the corner of a long table in a beautiful old hall. I woke up one morning and decided to turn our old living room into her dining room. For some reason, I felt the need to recreate this room for her for us. The house was already from an earlier period, so it showcased the proper wood trim finishings and hardwood floor. I stripped the walls of old paper and painted them dark red from the ceiling to two-thirds down. I added a chair rail and went out hunting for a black, wrought iron candle chandelier. I found someone to place Anaglypta, embossed paper, on the ceiling to give it a tin effect. I went out and bought an antique dining room set with a table, chairs, and a butler's table, and there you go. A few old Parisian prints and voila!

It was one way to get all of us together every Sunday. My parents had their own busy lives. Sunday was a good time for all of us. Leo's parents were older, so we included them always. I loved that family time. And I needed it desperately. Thank you, Sarah.

Mountains out of molehills

Have you ever heard that saying, "you are making a mountain out of a molehill." That was Leo. I always saw the molehill, and he saw the mountain. We were all under Leo's spell of guilt: stay active, be healthy, play sports, never quit. A few years later, after we put gymnastics on the back burner, I found my Elizabeth crying at the kitchen table. Her dad was sitting across from her.

"Dad wants me to run cross country, and I don't want to," she said.

"Her sisters ran cross country, and now it's her turn," Leo said. "She can't quit halfway through."

He and I were assistant trainers. Maybe it looked terrible on him. I spoke up, "If she's having problems with her knees, then I think it's up to her, don't you?"

It was time for the guilt train to hit the station. "You never take my side," he said. "She quit gymnastics. If she quits cross country, this will become a habit of hers."

"She's made her decision," I said and walked away.

With him, there was only one side to the story: his. It was that or had it rubbed in your face forever. We had a lot of those idiotic discussions in our household.

He found a small bag of weed in one of the kids' rooms once. They said it was their cousin's, and it was. I believed them. He didn't. Of course. He lost all trust in us like it was four against one. But who permitted him to go through their rooms? They were young adults by this point and good kids, but Leo still had control over them. Making the right decision wasn't always the right decision for you, but it was to appease dad. -Another red flag.

26

CHAPTER TWENTY-SIX:
My Parents Killed the Dog

I t was a Monday, and I thought I'd take a chance and ask my parents if they could watch the kids. We had a meeting at the school, and we both had to be there. They said yes, which was a surprise.

My parents were not your typical grandparents. They loved my girls, but they both worked full-time and had a life. Most of the time, when we needed a sitter, I paid for one. That's fine. It wasn't their thing. I just thought of being less than a mile away; they would enjoy spending time with the girls. I'm not sure why, except I do remember my mom's friend Diane complaining to my mom about how she had to watch her grandkids day and night. My mom kept saying over and over, "There's no way in hell I'm going to babysit my grandkids that much." She talked herself right out of it. Anyway, I needed help and couldn't get a sitter. My parents came over. I had to give mom full instructions on bedtime, bath time, and what to do with the dog.

Remember I had a turtle; this can't end well.

When we arrived back home, we found the corn broom eaten up on the front porch. *Wow, that's weird. Maybe it was the puppy.* We went inside, where my dad was asleep on the sofa. When I asked him where the dog was, he said, "I think he's outside in the back." Nope, no dog to be found. I went upstairs. My mother was still finishing up with the kids' bedtime. She hadn't seen the dog either, but she'd been upstairs the whole time. I went back downstairs and called the Humane Society. It's not unusual for dogs to be picked up in our neighborhood. Our old dog was picked up a few times after wondering off.

I called, and they said, "Yes, we have your dog, no need to retrieve him; we can just cremate him here for fifty bucks." "Do you want his collar back?".

They proceeded to tell me that he had sustained head injuries and passed away quickly. A young female driver had hit him in front of the house, and the neighbors called the Humane Society. They'd knocked on my door, but no one answered — bloody hell. Jack got out of the back yard and ran out onto the busy street, and this poor girl hit him. I felt terrible for her because no one was there to support her. I told them to keep the collar and hung up. I then turned and looked at my parents and said, "You killed the dog. You need to go home now."

I thought it was time for a good "Dogs go to Heaven "story, in case we were going to go through them like fish. I sat them down and started, "Ladies, did you know, every-time a child floats up to heaven, God gives them a gift of a pet, so they won't be alone when they enter the pearly gates. There are no real dogs in heaven; they're angels like Granma and Grampa. When a dog passes away, like your own, he becomes an angel, God gives him wings, and up he goes into the arms of a child".

Did you know Fish go to heaven as well?

I Killed the Fish

I was always taking care of the fucking fish tank with huge goldfish and small betta fish in it. Like moms have nothing better to do when they have thirty minutes for themselves. *Let's see, do my nails or clean up fish shit?* Never buy your young children a pet if they can't take care of it! I had a turtle when I was a kid. That was my pet. He got out of his tank, flipped himself over, and proceeded to dry up under the sofa.

One day I was cleaning the massive tank and I just cracked. I'd had enough. I dumped the goldfish into a pail, took them down the bank, and poured them into the pond behind us. Process of elimination. Fish first, and if that was easy, then the husband.

Madison's betta fish wasn't doing well, so I did what any mother would overfeed, swirl the water to see if it would come back to life. There was movement, maybe another week on this planet. I will put off the ceremony to fishy heaven for now.

The three girls watched me dump the container of dirty fish water into the bathroom sink. I thought I'd pushed down the drain plug before I started. Oops! Before I knew it, that damn fish was taking a ride on a wave of dirty water, heading for the drain. Round and round he went like a corkscrew water slide. I reacted quickly. I pushed the plunger down so the fish wouldn't be lost in the plumbing of hell. My reaction time-lagged a bit, and I proceeded to decapitate that sick fish with the drain plunger. Shrieks galore. I told them the fish had a brain tumor and had to be put out of its misery. I then suggested we go to Pet Smart and get another betta fish. Damn, here we go again.

27

CHAPTER TWENTY-SEVEN:

Why We Stay

*I*t should read, "Why we shouldn't stay," we stay for all the wrong reasons. Women are full of excuses as to why they remain in an unhappy marriage. We all do it. When I save up enough, I will leave. When the kids get older, I will go. When I can afford it, When I find a place to live, when Hell freezes over, I will go. I'm not important; my family's happiness comes first. Where is our mind at the time? Not in the present but the past, fueling the fire.

Change is scary. What we know, even if it's not healthy, is still our comfortable constant. Women have many excuses to avoid the inevitable. They ask themselves, "Am I going to divide up the perfect family picture, for my happiness? How dare I! How dare I or am I just a coward in disguise?

The funny thing is everyone saw through us. Women in my situation will tell themselves they can do one more day, week, month, or year, but eventually, when you bottom out, you hate who you have become. You explode! And some women still don't leave. Shame, fear, failure is all part of their vocabulary. I like this quote by Michelle Obama: *"There is no limit to what we, as women, can accomplish."*

It's incredible how we can create this busy, full, beautiful life around us and be so empty on the inside. It truly starts within you. I believe we are all born with a warm flame of love, and once it's extinguished, you're left with just a shell. You've lost your soul, and it feels like it won't come back. But it can and does come back. I'm proof of that.

You never do know what goes on behind closed doors.

Just Play the Game

Why are we locking the liquor cabinet, Leo? I understand the girls are not of age to drink, but why lock it? Just tell them it's your booze and keep your paws off the goods. Plus, the lock is so tiny, if the booze bandit were any more substantial then a mouse, they would be able to crack it open. He kept the key above in the glass cabinet, in a shot glass. Nobody would ever find that, lol. Like he was setting them up for failure and waiting for one of them to break into it. So he could discipline and be right, again. There was nothing good in there to steal anyway. He never bought hard liquor. If the girls were into bourbon or Black Velvet Whiskey, we were in trouble. Why instill a curiosity or an, *I do not trust you*, with this lock?

I think they did get into it, during their trial and error teenage phase. Usually throwing it up through your nostrils puts an end to that mischief. Some take a little longer with a variety of bevies. I always said, *"be careful about your choice of beverage, what you throw-up now, you will never choose to drink again. I'm talking violently ill"*. Mine's peppermint Schnapps and whiskey, made out ok.

This locking of the cabinet was a sign. Leo didn't trust people; he didn't trust his family. He created sneaky children. That wasn't healthy.

As time passed, we found ourselves all walking on eggshells around my husband. Asking for anything felt suffocating. I felt like a teenager asking to borrow Dad's brand-new car. He was still angry when I asked for time away with my girlfriends. I think he feared that they would talk me into leaving. I was way ahead of him on that one. He'd throw me the guilt-trip, but it wasn't working anymore. I was getting mentally stronger. The kids noticed a change in their father. They learned to play the game as well.

I loved my job, but I started to resent the new owner of the practice. Like my husband, he was a control freak. He micromanaged us like Leo did at home. Whatever I made in practice was never enough for the larger items we wanted for the house. I taught my fitness classes, which helped purchase my antique dining room set. My paycheque went to groceries, kids' activities, and their other needs. I was doing my part to be equal. Why didn't I feel like one?

I felt like the oldest daughter asking for a few bucks when I was short. I hated the position he put me in, that I put myself in. We created this situation together. The parent-daughter relationship never dissipated. If anything, as my daughters grew up, I realized that he treated me like one of them. He spoke down to me on a lower level.

So, what am I teaching my girls? What kind of role model am I for my children? I don't want my daughters to mirror my relationship actions. Do as I say, not as I do. I taught my girls to be kind to one another, respect their bodies, be physically active for their body and mind, but what about their mental health? No wonder women lose themselves. Their self-esteem flies out the window. How will they learn communication skills when we don't express ourselves adequately as parents? Living being two masks.

I take partial responsibility for letting it go that long. I left once, in the beginning, then I returned. That was so long ago. I looked in the mirror and was ashamed of the person I had become. *This person was a stranger. She was weak. I am a failure in this relationship, but there's still time.*

The guilty TRIP!

As a staff, we were saving our bonus money to go on a trip to Hawaii. We had a lunch meeting one day and were given two choices: We could go alone and use our bonus to enjoy the Hawaiian Islands or bring our significant other but have no spending money. We all went home and discussed this with our partners. Was I selfish to want to go and enjoy the trip with my staff? That was my accomplishment, my big trip, not his.

The next day at our meeting, we had a show of hands of who was bringing their partner. I was the only one with my hand up. Bloody hell, this trip was going to be miserable. I worked so hard for that staff bonus for everyone, and I had to be with my husband. What the fuck? But again, I swallowed and pressed on- The very last brick!

I would have to entertain him while my staff enjoyed the convention and each other. I had no choice. He should have said, "You've worked hard for that money, go and enjoy it." But instead, he said, "We never get to go away together. It will be fun." Really? I didn't have the strength or balls to fight him. I hated who I'd become. Either he was hoping to rekindle our relationship, or he didn't trust me and had to tag along — the spy who loved me scenario.

He took all my hard work and buried it in his selfishness. I hated him for that (another brick on my shoulders). But I hated myself at the same time for not standing up for myself. I should have just said, *"it's a working holiday, I worked hard for it, and I'm going."* Please don't make this about you and don't make me feel guilty, it won't work". But I didn't, and he went with me. Again, I tried very hard not to feed him to the sharks or push him into a volcano. He was melting my soul like Frosty the Snowman on a hot, sandy beach. Wasn't I killing his?

I heard that line over and over during my twenty-four-year marriage. It was practically tattooed on the back of my head. Though I doubted myself often, I realized that the selfish act is not to leave but to guilt someone into staying. Those people are selfish ones. I wasn't in love with anyone else, and I was in love with myself, and I needed to take care of her. I need me back.

I wanted to love another again, one day. Was I capable? I needed to breathe, and right then it felt like my head was being held underwater. There were plenty of times when I just wanted to get my car and keep going until I ended up somewhere with a sunset. I kept telling him that I was going to leave, and he would say, "Why don't you pack up and head to Australia? You always wanted to go there." Exactly, I did want to go there, but with our family on a job exchange. That was when the kids were younger. I suggested it, but he said no. Of course, he said no. What was I thinking, wrong person, wrong life, wrong time? My daughters did make it to Australia, and so did I. That's for another time.

It takes two to tango. Maybe we were both victims of this marriage. But it was time to finish this dance. You can only make yourself happy. I realize that now. You cannot be responsible for someone else's happiness. I know it takes two to tango, and I'm at as much fault for this failed relationship as him. At that point, it was, do, or die for me. He wasn't going anywhere, and he made that quite clear from the beginning. My girlfriend said, "do not leave the matrimonial home until you have papers signed."

Throughout our marriage, I had the opportunity to cheat on him. We all do, but we make choices, the right decision in marriage is not to. But I was accused of it always. I just needed to feel human, to explore some emotional loving, and to give it back. But I'd agreed from the beginning to be faithful to him, and I was. When I would withdraw from him, he'd think I was unfaithful. As I said before, I could not have any male friends. Anytime a guy looked at me or approached me, Leo was down my throat—his insecurity, not mine. I spent years explaining myself to him. Goodness, that's bloody exhausting.

I wanted something in my life, anything to make me feel alive again. Was I even capable of loving someone, genuinely loving them wholeheartedly? I never had. I had a high school crush, maybe, but that was it. I'd look in the mirror and start questioning my mortality. I thought, *Maybe I like women! I fit the stereotypical a tomboy, and I loads of girlfriends, play hockey, and hated men. I think women are sexier than men, and at this point, maybe I should switch teams. I have absolutely no interest in men whatsoever. Men in my books were garbage. There was a control button on the back of my head, and they pushed it regularly, at work and home.*

I had a close friend from another high school when I was younger. He went off to university, and I met and married Leo. He'd see me every so often and ask how I was. I romantically thought nothing of him, he was just a friend—but I thought to myself, I'm in a very vulnerable state, and marriage is on thin ice, don't talk to me. I'll have to explain myself. Leo was the jealous type. I don't think he ever trusted me. Sad really to live like there were a set of eyes piercing the back of your head.

I was at a point in my marriage where we were nothing but room-mates. I'd been looking secretly for a place to live for over a year. I started talking more and more to this old friend of mine.

He wasn't happy either, married to a bossy woman. It felt good to have a conversation with a reasonable person who seemed to understand me. We had common ground. He had his demons, though, and I was in no emotional state to help him with his issues. What was I thinking, anyway? I was in a bad headspace, hating men. Why would I even start a conversation or anything else with one?

I knew I was on my way out of the marriage. It was great to confide in someone who felt like I did. Leo thought I was having a torrid affair with this person. Who's got time for that, and my hatred for ALL men were growing inside of me. We sent emails back and forth and a few phone conversations. We met in private to talk a few times. You see, if I were allowed to have kept my guy friends, I would not have felt like I had to sneak around behind Leos back to talk to this person. He thought it was about sex, because where most men's minds are, in the gutter.

Meeting a male friend for a beer, in public, is not heard of in my world.

Before I could end something that never started, Leo found our emails and phone conversations. I wish I had acted on any advancements this man showed towards me. I needed to feel love for someone, anyone, I felt empty and alone for so many years. Leo confronted me on the mes-sages, in our (his) hot-tub, which I hated. I denied the affair. Leo took it upon himself to meet this person where I was supposed to see him. Leo took the liberty of ending it for me. I never spoke to that friend again. I was so embarrassed. If that's not a control freak move on Leo's part, what is? I mean, I didn't belong to him. I wasn't his wife, only on paper. We were don. He had no right to finish what I was going to end anyway. How dare he!

That just sealed the deal. Leo made another mountain out of a mole-hill. He made every situation in that family about himself. He knew I was leaving and that we had a loveless marriage. We were living in separate rooms. Maybe for the sake of his pride, it was easier to say that his wife left him for another man than his wife left him because she never loved him.

I knew I had it in me to care for another human being and could care for another man one day, but it would take a long time. I had plenty of healing and self-discovery.

Circling the Drain

I'm melting. It's the middle of summer, and I'm melting inside. I found that I was talking to myself often. I had a love-hate relationship with myself. I loved myself inside, the old me, but I hated who I had become: a lonely, empty slave in his house to my husband. Always teaching us lessons. Making our failures about himself. He internalized everything. There was no partnership here. I saw other husbands pulling their weight, so why not mine? I think we dive into our work and our homes to avoid that everlasting question: "Why am I not happy?"

One day Leo called my oldest daughter and myself over for a family conference. The day's lesson was cell phone use. We had a family plan like most families. He said she and I were using up our data too quickly and I should hand my phone in. First of all, if we're using up too much data, we will buy more—we had a family plan. Second, if our oldest is abusing her phone, feel free to take it away. I'm your wife, not your child, so please do not treat me like one. What the fuck was he talking about? *You want a woman, but you treat me like a child,* I thought to myself.

Big red flag!

I felt incomplete as a woman, as a lover, and as a partner. I couldn't give him that piece of me because it wasn't there, it wasn't his. My cup was always half full. I always thought, and still do, that things could be worse. I was lucky to have my health, my family's health, live in a beautiful country, and wake up every day to a great cup of coffee. Enjoy what life has to offer simplicity. I worked hard around the house to avoid the inevitable.

I would spend my day off pulling weeds from the rolling bank we had. I needed a couple of goats. I tried plants and rocks to create a landscape of some sort. I just kept busy. At times I felt terrible for him. He'd come home wanting to take the family out for dinner, and the kids would say no thanks, they were busy. They were getting older and had their friends and plans. Bloody Hell that would leave just me and him. Now in another world, a happy couple would be thankful that their kids were all heading out for the night, doing the happy dance, but towards the end, that time was just downright awkward.

I felt I was in a controlled marriage trapped in his world. Sometimes I would break down crying in the shower. What was that all about? They say you use up the same amount of energy laughing as you do to cry. I had to decide early on in my journey to be as happy as I could be. He wasn't a bad man. He never hit the kids or me; it was all mental. Those bruises take a very long time to go away, and sometimes they never do. I still have to remind myself not to "ask" for an evening out with a girl-friend, but a considerate mention.

I worked in the public eye regularly, and I was good at taking any awkward situation and turning it into a joke. Why not laugh through life? I look back now and can't believe how you can take something so sad, so awkward, and make it so bloody funny. I think they call this the Band-Aid effect, but after time, the Band-Aid falls off, and a festering wound needs your attention before infection sets in. I needed out, and soon for both our sakes.

27

CHAPTER TWENTY-SEVEN:

'Til Death Do You Part

*H*ow the hell did I get here without taking my own life, or his? Let's go back to that line, "'til death do you part." I thought they said that, so you'd stay together and grow old together. When one passed, the other would be left apart. Your heart was whole and was left in half. I'm sure that's what that line meant. But in my life, it took on a whole new meaning. Our marriage lacked trust. I don't think he ever really trusted me since I left the first time. Why did he want me back so badly? Maybe I would ruin the picture he'd painted of us. I think he knew deep down that I never loved him in that way, and we were never meant to be together. But then, I look at our three angels, and I wouldn't have done anything differently. They were meant to be here and to be ours. How could I get out of this mess without a financial fight? I couldn't kill him or myself—that would break up the family unit. Still, I was exhausted, and desperate times require desperate measures. I needed someone to take care of me, to meet my emotional needs, and I in-turn reciprocate.

Jail started to seem pretty good. Think of it: I'd be in prison, but someone else would be cooking three square meals for me. I'd have one outfit a day and someone to do my laundry. I could read all the books I wanted. Maybe I'd finish a university degree, like so many others, and have my schooling paid. I could always get out early on good behavior.

That's not a bad gig. I could still watch my kids grow up. Too bad prison food is so atrocious.

28

Chapter Twenty-Eight:
My aha moment

*L*eo blamed me for his unhappiness. And he's partially true. We were like a business, and he provided the roof, I offered the services inside the establishment. I didn't want to make him happy or sad, and I didn't want him to feel anything for me. He would say, "If you're so miserable, why don't you leave and go find your happiness? But you won't be able to manage by yourself. You'll never find anyone who loved you as much as I did and provided for you as I did." *Try me!* I thought to myself.

"It's just a house, Leo," I'd reply. "Four walls and a roof—that's it." *I'm leaving you and thihouse. It was my prison for years. You're like a 160-pound tumor, and I'm cutting you out.*

One of my favorite movies is *Moulin Rouge*. Nicole Kidman sang, "One day, I'll fly away." Now was my time to fly.

In my head, that was me. I had it with this man, this marriage. I knew I was going to be okay. Make your own damn happy Leo I'm out. You cant control me if 'Im not here, or can you?

Maya Angelo once wrote; Control what you can; don't control what you can't control.

You can't control how people think, and their reactions to events, so don't even try. Take care of yourself, take care of your mental health.

I knew that if I didn't leave, I'd be spending our twenty-fifth anniversary in Greece, with a stranger. Like Gilligan, I would have left him on a small Greek island, without a paddle.

I discovered that as soon as you close one door in your mind and open another, the whole world looks different and brighter. I asked myself this question for the last time: What is wrong with me? I realized that absolutely nothing was wrong with me. I knew I had to get the fuck out of that house before I kill myself. My soul was already there. It was poison being there. When your teenage children tell you to leave, that they will be fine, then you know it's time to go.

During one of my last visits to our counselor, he was asking questions stemming from Leo's desperation over my leaving.

Nothing had changed inside of e emotionally, and I felt the same about him from the first time we were here twenty-two years ago. Emotionally empty. I had nothing in me to give.

The councilor, same dude we had last time, three marriages in, begins;

"If Leo sold the family house and you bought a house together, would you stay?"

"No."

"If Leo bought you your engagement ring, something you could pick out yourself, would you stay?"

"No."

If Leo gave you more responsibility over the banking, would you stay?"

"Hell no." In my head I was screaming, *OMG folks, IT'S TOO LATE TO SAVE THIS LOVELESS MARRIAGE!*

I got up from the sofa, looked straight at Leo, and said, "You should stay; you need plenty of help." And I walked out.

You can't stay in a one-sided, heartless relationship, can you? Your soul will die. We're here for one reason: to be loved and spread the love. Instead, we choose to bury our feelings and live a lie, and it slowly kills us inside. I would go on, day to day, loving my kids, and protecting them.

I wasn't living our life, our dream—it was only his. I realized that the negative vibe he was always putting out was melting my soul. I know now that you can only make yourself happy. I wasn't a problem, but I could be part of the solution. And honestly, it was about my happiness, but it was about his too. I knew he needed to come to terms with his roots—or lack thereof. I could sense his insecurities coming from his past. He needed to figure that one out for himself.

Planet of the Apes

Evolution. We are primates like the ape. We share genetic similarities. They say we originated from apelike ancestors six million years ago. Think about it, four million years ago, in Africa, we stood upright and walked on two legs. Much easier for running a marathon. No more bloody knuckles. They had enormous heads that they carried on those hunched back shoulders, holding their baseball bat in case there was a fight to be had. Their arms were still too long, and they dragged their fingers on the ground when they moved. These ape-like creatures gathered, hunted, fished, and provided for their family. They pulled their women around by the hair, to keep her from milling about into other caves. She was his procession. Do you see the pattern here? They needed to feel, important, wanted, and they must be providers for their family, or they are a failure in today's society. Was Leo a caveman? Did evolution play a considerable role in my failed marriage? Think about it, if female primates dominated those caves, dragged their men around by their balls, we would have a female President and Priminister by now. What a different world we would all be living in. It wouldn't be about greed, power, pride, and money but about, love, sharing, nurturing, and equality.

It was just a thought I had. I like to paint a different picture of women.

I Am Woman, Hear Me Roar

I was having a Helen Reddy flashback. Goodness, I'm getting old. When she first sang that song on stage, it was 1971. When girl-power was coming on strong. When women had something to say. I was 7. Helen sings, "Yes I am wise, but its wisdom born of pain, yes I've paid the price, but look how much I've gained".

Ok, the song was a little nasally, but the words were profound. My experiences made me stronger and feel invincible, like I can do anything. If you ever need a song to lift your spirits, when you made to feel less than you are, play Helen's song. You must sing it out load into the mirror, make sure you are listening.

Until I left, I stayed positive. I had to swallow that rush of guilty stomach bile. It would enter the back of my throat and burn me whenever I had a confrontation with Leo. That lasted a few years. Nothing goes away overnight but the tumor. I still had my emotional stability to take care of.

I joined a boxing club. I needed to hit something. My goodness, it felt great taking my anger and aggression out on a heavy bag. I surrounded myself with positive people and would do things that made me happy. I had a huge friend base. I'd continue teaching my fitness classes, as they were an excellent distraction. We'd have a ladies' night out. I called those evenings, "the Stitch and Bitch night." It had nothing to do with sewing. Some wine loosened up the conversation, allowing friends to open up their hearts and souls. A book club without the book. We had our storyline. We are our therapy. Women do better in a pack: book clubs, fitness classes, craft nights. Call it what you want, we enjoy that time together. It's in our DNA.

If you're strong enough to listen to your heart, and if you have family or friends standing behind you, then you will make it out. If you believe that this is not going to go on forever and that there is happiness at the end of the tunnel, then allow yourself that peace. That rainbow does exist, and not just through a glass of Chardonnay.

His world was crumbling, and I felt I was the cause of it. He was taking no ownership for the lose of this marriage. I hated to hurt him, but there were no other options. Maybe if he knew his roots, perhaps it would have been different. Knowing you might have siblings out there would bring comfort and stability, but he never wanted to find out. Living with a person who isn't happy will suck the happiness right out of your life. It's a lot of work for the other parent to have to overcompensate for that. Your children will suffer too. I know this for a fact. If you're going to leave, do it when the kids are younger. Then they still have time to form their own identities.

He wasn't leaving the family home, this canvas of sadness and broken dreams. I knew that from the beginning. I had to go. After his father passed away, I moved into his dad's suit that we'd built onto the house. I could get my space there until I found a place close to the bus route so that I could share the parental duties. I needed a lawyer and a separation before I could leave. My girlfriend advised me of that. I needed a plan. I went once, too fast, without thinking, not this time, 24 years later, I'm doing it the right way and taking care of my needs.

After that summer, dynamics changed drastically for everyone. Alix went off to university, so she was out of town in Toronto. We moved her into the residence. I knew she was hurting, but what could I do? I know now that the timing sucked. But there's never a good time to leave your family home.

Alix recently told me that she felt pressured to go away to university. Leo was from the old- school way of thinking. He would say, "If they don't go to university right after high school, they will never go." This way of thinking is so foolish. But again I spoke up once and got shot down like a fighter pilot.

"I don't believe that for a minute," I'd reply. "These kids graduate high school at seventeen, and not all of them know what they want at that age. What about community college, or working for a couple of years first?"

It was Leo's way or the highway. We were pawns on his chessboard; it was always Leo's move. We just played the game!

Alix thrived in the big city. Her experience was good, but there was a lot of unresolved emotional trash we had to work through. That may take years to sort out. Alix was away, so she was forgotten, in my eyes. Her sisters were still in high school, and they received counseling.

I taught my girls to be tough and street smart, to see the world and take all that life has given you and give back. Life is a gift, and it's short, so don't waste it. The girls were becoming young adults and would have to form a new relationship with their dad from then on.

My work was suffering. I had a hard time working with the new owner of the practice. He was a micromanaging, control freak as well. My job was to make him money, but I was in a different headspace. I hated how men made me feel. I couldn't stay in that practice anymore. The staff was taking sides, and we weren't a team anymore. He hired a girl-Friday, she set up her office beside his. She was his permanent ass licker and stroker when he required reassurance that, *Doggie Hausser,* another young doctor reference, was doing a good job. It wasn't a healthy workplace for me. My job was to market the practice and make money for this guy. Why? I couldn't be that hamster spinning someone else's magic wheel of cash. It was time to leave.

After twenty-four years, I left my husband and my job and took with me all my wonderful memories and friendships that I carry close to my heart. I left physically and mentally. I never go backward. I feel like I killed two birds with one stone. Both were holding me back. I didn't like either man in my life, my husband or my new boss. They both left a bad taste in my mouth. It's time to create my canvas.

29

CHAPTER TWENTY-NINE:

Escaped His Painting

I was living in the in-law suite until I moved out. Before I moved out, for his birthday, I gave Leo a beautiful watercolor I had done for him. In over twenty-four years the house was never completed. I asked one thing only—finish the front steps with a country look to match the porch. It never happened. I don't gt it. The cement steps are still there. Bloody stubborn!

So, I found a local artist to finish it in a beautiful watercolor. As I said in the beginning, I felt like I was trapped in a painting, a vision—his vision of what was the perfect family. You never know what goes on behind closed doors, do you? I also wanted to see it completed.

The artist completed the renovations in a painting. She did a fabulous job, the way I wanted it done. I had her put three sets of eyes in the upstairs windows, representing the kids, and a set of eyes through the fence to represent the dog.

I was not in the painting. I didn't belong there. It wasn't my place anymore. It never was. It was time to start my canvas — time to start my journey. Towards the end of our marriage, the air was thick, almost unbreathable. We socked away some great memories in that house and raised three beautiful angels, but after twenty-four years, there had to be both good and bad, right? I had to go through what I did to get to this point, to get to the next stage in life.

I was free, but was I damaged goods? I wondered if I would ever find myself again. I felt like I had left my daughters there to fend for themselves. Would they ever be free mentally? It was going to take some serious soul searching to smooth over the guilt I felt, but I knew it would be worth it. My guilt, was to his benefit, financially. I just wanted out, I should have taken more, but I didn't. My lawyer thought I was crazy being so kind, coming from such a long marriage. But why piss Leo off. The ball was in court. He had to sign off on the papers, for me to get another home close by. I played the game.

The Sound of Music

I felt like Julie Andrews in *The Sound of Music*. The four of us girls used to dance around the family room singing all her songs. I imagined all of us (the von Trapp Family) dressed in our best peasant dresses, arms stretched out, twirling around and singing on top of a hillside of the Austrian Alps. Now, where was my Captain?

I was free, but even freedom has a price tag. I didn't consider how I would feel leaving that home. It had been my home since I was eighteen. That's all I knew. Leo was never selling the house; he made that very clear. So, there was no division of household goods.

I asked if he could take the kids and leave for a few hours so I could get my belongings. Again, he didn't trust me. My new place was two streets over. I grabbed a friend's truck and headed over. It was the first time I was back at the house since I'd left.

I pulled in that driveway, walked up the steps, and knocked on the door. Even though my touches were everywhere, I was now a real stranger in someone else's home. It looked familiar but distant. Leo and the girls were sitting at the kitchen table when I walked in.I'm not surprised. I asked him to remove the kids before I came, so they wouldn't see the look in my eyes when I was getting the rest of my things. He didn't give a shit, and he loved it. He had that smug look. I know what he was thinking. *Look at your rotten mother, leaving us to fend for ourselves, shes so cruel, but she deserves everything she's got coming to her.* I felt like I was the one going off to school. I'm sure the Gestapo was briefing the soldiers before my arrival. I went straight upstairs to gather my things. When I came down, I took a few pictures off the wall — my memories of the girls growing up. I was in a weird headspace, feeling sad, happy, very awkward.

Our wedding picture was gone. I found that smashed into pieces in the garbage. I grabbed all the kids' artwork, letters, and cards they'd given us over the years. Everything else was just stuff. It meant nothing. That Christmas I gave the girls each a scrapbook of our family's memories.

I walked back into the kitchen, swallowing my tears. I didn't want to upset the girls. I was going through the motions. I grabbed a spatula, a wooden spoon, and a frying pan. In my mind, I walked right over to Leo. I was going to wipe the smirk off his face with the bottom of the cast iron pan, peeled his face off the bottom and left.

I had to get out of there. I ran that house for twenty-four years, and I was suddenly in an awkward position and made to feel guilty again, like an outsider. I look back at that moment now and cringe at the person he tried to make me. His trophy for all his friends to appreciate.

I grabbed a few more small items and left. What else could I remove from the family home where they were all still living? The toaster, the coffee maker, maybe the toilet? I kick myself now for not taking my hot tub. I will never be put in that situation again. Ever! I came back later, in the middle of the night, to claim a picture off my dining room wall that I loved. A Paris café. *I will see that in person one day,* I said to myself. I was going to miss that room.

Good-bye Sarah!

I'm gone physically, but will I ever be gone mentally?

Pic two old ladies hugging:

Thelma and Louise (girl power)

We all have them. Our besties. Women that we connect with. Women who we can confide in and not feel like your being judged. It's usually not a sibling but a soul you met along the way. Mine is Thelma. She knows who she is. We laugh, we cry, we drink, we watch chick flicks together, and I know she's got my back through thick and thin. And I have hers. Thelma is almost angelic. She is a selfless, giving person, puts everyone's needs ahead of hers. If they did a remake of *Charlie's Angels*, she would be the smart Farrah, and she has the hair to prove it. We have spent years tugging at each other's paintings, trying to peel each other off the mutilated canvas we have created. It's been messy for both of us. I know I'm speaking for thousands of women out there who have these souls in their life. We are blessed to have them.

We have both visited our mediums at different stages of the game. I think I introduced Thelma to her first channel. She has seen a few since. In one of her readings, she was told her son would have a family with a set of twins to boot. Over drinks years later, we confided in each other's past readings. It was a jaw-dropping moment. I was also told one of my daughters would give birth to twins as they are in my family as well. We always spoke of being grandparents together, now with our children that would sweet. Time will tell.

I invite Thelma over or a drink after work. Leo was still annoying me to no end. I thought after we separated, moved out of the family home, he would cut me some slack. I lived too close and convenient for him. I was always the emotional wall for both of us. We poured drinks and sat outside. We made small talk, and then the flood gates opened. I just started wailing. I could stop. Years and years of emotion came pouring out like Niagara Falls.

Thelma comforted me and said, "OMG your human, cry my friend, I am here for you."

One day we will do that road trip, convertible top-down, wind in our air, laughing all the way.

For now, it's one day a time.

There's a light at the end of the tunnel with you in my life.

Love you, Thelma.

30

CHAPTER THIRTY:

The Dating Game

I was living two streets down from the family home and finally taking care of myself, managing my own home, and doing a pretty good job of it. The best thing was that it was a quarter of the size and, no rolling bank of weed. On cleaning day, I would open the front and back doors and let the wind carry my dust-balls out into the streets. It's perfect. Quasimodo had officially retired. Ring your own fucking bell.

I did nothing for the first year. I made a beautiful place for the girls, read some self-help books, cooked for my kids, and exhaled. I was still dealing with Leo's games, but I had my home to escape too. My friend was on a dating site and created a profile for me. *Okay*, I thought. *I'll give it a try. Let's see, what am I looking for in a man? He should be my age or younger, take care of his body and self-image. If he looks nine months pregnant, forget it. I wonder what's out there. Let's give it a try.*

At first, I just deleted anyone who contacted me. I wasn't ready and, honestly, I indeed had been through a lot. I hated men. If one knocked on my door and pissed me off, look out, I will do one better then Lorraine Bobbit, and I will use my Magic Bullet! You see where my headspace was. We need to take time for ourselves to be still, be in the present. Find out who we are.

Months later, I received a message in my inbox. John Doe had an excellent profile, and he was cute, single and no baggage—I hoped. Have you ever been to a bar and spotted the married man picking up younger girls? You can tell from the wedding band finger tanned from playing golf. It's sad. Well, I messaged back, and we kept up the banter for a couple of weeks. He liked what I like, and he enjoyed what I enjoy. It seemed perfect.

We agreed to meet for a drink. That week, before the date, I found a rose in my mailbox. He messaged me and said, "A rose for a beautiful woman." That's strange. How did the mystery guy get my address? I don't think I gave it to him. That was a red flag. Was I paranoid?

He covered up nicely in an email, so I kept the date to meet him for that drink, but in the back of my mind, I thought, *this guy is too good to be true. How does he know where I live?* There are a lot of creeps out there—I know, I was married to one. Time to get ready for my big date. What do I wear? I called my daughters, and they came over to help mom get ready. They were as excited as I was. Finally after all these years, moms getting out. I was sitting at the bar having a drink, eager to meet my mystery man, but after my first glass of wine, I realized he was a no show.

Really? Was I stood up? "Bloody hell, that's it! Do guys stand you up in this day and age, without a text? No way. I know who this mystery man is, my ex!" He was very calculating, he knew too much about me, and my daughter just received graduation roses. I had my kids do a little investigating on the computer and cunted the roses. Leo was chatting with me for a month, and a rose was missing. That idiot wouldn't leave me alone. I'd had enough! I sent Leo a text later when my kids dropped me back off at home. I knew he was at the show with his girlfriend (yes, he had moved on). It read, "My date was a no show. You were right—I hate online dating. Why don't you drop in for a drink?" I was cracking up. I couldn't hold it together.

There were so many emotions running through my head.

I can only handle so much bullshit. I called my girlfriend to come over. I told her that if she didn't show up quickly, it would be off with his penis when he walked in the door. My magic bullet was waiting. When she walked in the door, I was drinking straight out of the bottle and holding a large knife. He drove by slowly just after that and didn't stop. I can now see how people leave their bodies and go berzerk. You have this insane moment you have no control over. You just snap.. It's like when you hear a person give their statement in the courtroom. The lawyer will ask," How do you not remember chopping him up into little pieces on the lawn?" You don't. You go insane temporarily, I guess. But now I can see how it happens to people. You can only handle so much stress. We all have a tipping point.

The next day, Leo sent me an email confirming what I already knew; it was he who stood me up. He was my blind date. He also said, " you are those girl's mother, how can you date strangers, they could chop you up into pieces and put you into a box." There is a lot of chopping going on here. Pent up anger on both sides.

It was a long while before I tried the dating game again. Are they all idiots? It couldn't get any worse. How else do you meet people with a busy schedule, at the grocery store? Here's a funny dating story: I met a guy for a drink, and we had a lovely time exchanging little facts about each other. After that drink, I said goodbye. He called for a second date a week later. We agreed to meet at seven o'clock one night. I was at the bar enjoying the bartender's banter and realized that an hour had gone by. I was stood up again, but this time I knew it wasn't my ex. Maybe he got into an accident. I was worried, but I left to go home. I figured he'd message me one day. Five days went by before he called me with his story: His live-in girlfriend had returned, while he was in the shower. Girlfriend! She'd read his messages and was furious. She took his phone, wallet, and car keys away from him and drove off. Good for her. He then proceeded to ask if we could try again next week. I was like, "Are you kidding me? You have a girlfriend!" She did me a favor.

On another date, the guy started firing off a line of questions at me. I felt like I was in a job interview. I left before my drink was done. I told him, "Those questions are not appropriate for a first date. That's why you're still single." Ciao, amigo.

I decided to take a break. If I needed sex, I had my fabulous Cadillac of vibrators and my good old showerhead. A single woman requires those items in her home—that and a reserve of wine.

31

CHAPTER THIRTY-ONE:

Glutton for punishment

*N*ow I know what people were saying, when they said, "Emily you're a Glutton for punishment." I did take on too much. That's for sure. Who doesn't when you have a busy life? Did I make time for me? We had a soaker tub, how many bathes did I have? Did I keep my life so moving for a reason? Was I afraid to be along, to be still, in silence? I enjoyed a good book and a quiet walk but to be in the moment, present and silent? Maybe I was scared to be alone, afraid of who I might find. To find out what makes Emily tick.

Leaving the family home was the first step to silence. My street was quiet, and the house was calm when the kids were at their dad's. I had never been alone. Since I was eighteen, the life I had with Leo was all I knew. I started talking to myself, well I always did that in my head, but now it was out loud. I was in the produce section one day, a woman next to me said, "pardon, I didn't hear you." I replied, "I must be talking to myself again, sorry."

I made a pact with myself, to spend time with me, enjoy my own company. I read all those inspirational, self-help books, watched educational pod-casts. I sat in the tub with a glass of wine and a " word search" book. I'm going to ok, right?

It was time to get the house in order. My life took a couple more side trips, but first, I needed to take care of my furnace. It wasn't working, so

I contacted the furnace guy. He arrived shortly after the call. He fixed my furnace, took my cheque, and left. He called back an hour later and asked if he'd left his screwdriver behind. I laughed and replied, "Nope." My youngest daughter thought he was somewhat cute and making a pass at me. I immediately texted a girlfriend from work who lived out of town and was moving out West. I wanted to tell her that I was back in the game and that an adorable guy dropped in to repair and asked me out.

A text came back: "What kind of woman would let a total stranger into her home and then date him?"

Who the hell was this? I asked, and the person replied, "I'm Jeremy. Who are you?"

"Never mind me," I said. "Where's my girlfriend? Isn't this her number anymore?"

"Nope. I just moved to town and picked up this new number."

I'm not sure why I needed to speak with the person. We started communicating by text and then the odd phone call. He knew I was older and had older children, but he was wise beyond his years, single, and funny in a strange sort of way. I needed an adventure. Someone without baggage. No kids or an Ex-wife. We made that clear in the beginning, no facebook or photos. Didn't want looks to get in the way. A few weeks later, we agreed to meet at a local pub.

When I get a phone call. "Hello," I say. "It's Jeremy," he replied. "Oh, hi, where are you?" "Across the street, staring at you." I will be right over". I felt like I knew this person from somewhere before. Maybe another life. It wasn't awkward at all. We started to hang out as friends. He was a good distraction.

Leo never stopped badgering me about it. Why did he care? Jealous? Ownership issues? I created a lot of fire in his soul. Leo must feel he wasted a lifetime with me. But it wasn't a waste. We had plenty of Goodtimes and three beautiful children to show for it. I believe everything happens for a reason. We were supposed to have that journey together, if not to help each other out then to help someone else.

Ladders Are Tippy

My dad always said that if you're going to go up the ladder, make sure someone is down below to hold it. Those words came to me as I was falling to the ground. I landed on top of the metal ladder. I was fortunate to have my youngest daughter there, who called 911. I'd broken my wrist, busted my knee, and hurt my head. I was in shock, but being the mother, I am, I yelled to her, "Turn off the salmon dinner. That shit's expensive." I asked her to bring me something frozen from the freezer for my arm. She brought me a pound of butter. I told her we needed that for the salmon when we returned from the hospital. Grab the peas.

I knew that the EMS guys would cut my hoodie off, so I tried to remove it myself, but to no avail. It felt like I was pulling my hand off with it. I was going to pass out if they didn't get there soon.

My youngest ran down the street to direct the EMS to our place. I waited for hours at the hospital on heavy meds. It was busy that night. My parents showed up. My mom, the bossy nurse, was bugging the staff to take care of me. Remember, I was on morphine for the pain. Finally, at midnight, I pointed straight at my dad and said, "Take her home now." She wasn't helping. My dad scooped her up, and away they went.

It was after midnight before I was finally in with the orthopedic surgeon on call. He took one look at my X-ray and decided to put me under, reduce my wrist, and cast it. "See you next Thursday at my clinic." He snubbed me. He never thought of nerve damage. I lost the use of my dominant hand over that winter. I'm left-handed, and that's the hand that took the fall. By the time I had my third cast change, I had realized this guy knew nothing about my wrist. If I was ever going to save the hand, I needed a real specialist. My friend, who was the cast technician, told me to take all my records and run. I reported that orthopedic doctor to the College of Surgeons. He got his wrist slapped.

I went straight to Toronto, where my sister, a nurse, found an amazing, caring orthopedic surgeon in her hospital. He was my angel. He took one look at my limp hand and said he could fix it. I started crying.

I found myself unable to do my job and stuck in another cast. I asked the doctor if I could travel, and he agreed, so I went to London, England, to visit my youngest daughter, who was living there at the time. We spent a couple of weeks traveling. When I got back home, I realized I couldn't do my job anymore. I had limitations on feeling, movement, and strength in y dominant hand.

My girlfriend asked me to clean her home. "Sure," I replied. "I love to clean; it's therapy for me." She found me more work, and the word got out fast, so I made it a business, and it grew. I was working all over and enjoying the fact that I didn't have to answer to a man ever again. That alone was a very satisfying feeling. I knew it wasn't my forever. Nothing is. It was just another stepping-stone over the river of life.

A quote from T.S. Elliot

I live by this quote

"People to whom nothing has ever happened cannot understand the unimportance of events."

Some people ask me, "Do you ever ask yourself why these things always happen to you." I say, "No, I don't wait for them to happen. I expect things to happen. My life is a playground of adventure. You must live it not waste it. I put myself out there, and if you do nothing, nothing will happen. We get to go around once in this body, this vessel we have chosen. We have choices even before we come to this realm. I wanted this body I'm in, to keep up with my lifestyle. I live my life, so I take care of my body mentally and physically, and it will take care of me.

Car Accident

Less than two months later, while coming home from work, I hit black ice on the highway and smashed up my car. I spun across three lanes and ended up in the gravel. Thank goodness I still had a cast on my hand that kept all my pins in place. It could have been a lot worse. It must have been my angel again. Thank you, Aunt Betty. The airbag gave me a good wallop on the side of my head, and the front one never deployed.

There was a recall on that front airbag, but they never called me back to replace it. I was waiting for BMW, which you know stands Big, Money, Waste. It was an older model, but I thought I deserved it. I guess not. It gave me nothing but trouble. I had the car keyed from front to back, the soft top was knifed, and the driver's side key entry was damaged from an attempted break and entered. The vehicle went into lockdown. They had to break a window to get into it. I was not meant to have that vehicle. It had bad karma. If you don't know what Smudging is, it's when you clear that negative energy around you and usher in positive energy by burning a sage stick. I needed to smudge my entire life and start again.

The universe was telling me to slow down. Stop running, lady! You've been spinning your entire life. I needed a safe space, away from Leo and this small town. How was I ever going to start my painting, but I still felt trapped? I needed to jump off this hamster wheel.

32

CHAPTER THIRTY-TWO:

Living on a Roller Coaster

*A*fter a year or so, I rented out my little home to a young lady and her aunt. I left town and moved in with Jeremy and his two roommates. We could help each other out—share in the bills, hang out, and have some laughs. He lived with two other guys. That was an interesting dynamic, but it was pretty much uneventful. As soon as we'd hear the music for *Jeopardy*, we'd all rush to the living room. What a bunch of nerds. I loved it. They called me Penny, from *The Big Bang Theory* television show. We acquired a dog, and I brought my daughter's little pup with me. They soon became friends.

It took six months for me to realize that Jeremy had some depression issues. I could help him with that. There I went again, Mother Teresa. Then he got worse. He wouldn't get up for work or even call in sick; he'd stay in his room in the dark. He started drinking more and passing out early in the evening. People who hurt themselves have a mental illness. Jeremy required a doctor and professional help. Mental illness is an actual disease like cancer. There is no choice here. He told me once he has suffered since he was eight years old. Jeremy requires something I can't give him, therapy.

I'd had enough of this shit, but I had already rented out my place to a woman and her aunt. They had a year lease, so I'd have to find a place to live for a while. Jeremy and I were still friends. He was sweet and never abusive to me, but he had a mental illness and needed professional help.

He'd get angry, but it was never directed at me. He tried self-medicating with booze and drugs to deafen the voices in his head. We tried local counseling and anti-depressants with minimal results. I found him rolled up in a ball, crying, a few times. I couldn't do it anymore. I needed to move out. I'm trying to heal myself, but instead, I was punishing myself.

We agreed to keep our friendship but live apart. Jeremy moved closer to his work, and that's when I moved in with one of my girlfriends. We understood each other completely. She was awesome. I felt happy and safe there. No questions asked. He moved away and took the dogs with him. That's how we stayed in touch, through puppy visits on the weekends. We still enjoyed each other's company. His good days were great, but his bad days were miserable. We were still friends helping each other out.

I wasn't looking for a husband or a boyfriend. He was just a good friend, nothing serious. I wasn't ready to heal myself, so I diverted my energies to Jeremy. He was the total opposite of Leo. As women, we tend to do that after a long, unsuccessful relationship. Go from one extreme to the next. I did, anyway. I'd see him on the weekends, walk the dogs, do the gardens together, finish puzzles, play Scrabble, and cook. We just kept it simple. I felt if he needed me, I was there for him. His family was disappointed in him, and they thought he was acting out. But suicidal tendencies are serious business. Maybe I was being played me as well.

I knew one day my prince would come, but I wasn't ready for him.

My mother was so worried about me. "Emily, you're not getting any younger. How are you going to support yourself? You need to find a nice man."

"Bloody hell, Mom. I'm fine, and please find a new hobby." I knew I didn't want to be back in my hometown. It's a small city. People talk, and I'd done all I could there. I never go backward in life. Always forward.

Your Mother's a Bad Influence

We paint on canvas, and it's permanent. Why not your body? Our skin is the perfect canvas to express yourself. Leo and I had different opinions on things. He felt I was a bad influence on his children. I had a few respectful piercings, nothing in my brow, nose, or nipple. I waited for my first tattoo. I had wanted a one for a long time but had to wait until I moved out so that Leo (Dad) wouldn't be pissed. He probably thought. First, my first tattoo would lead to the kids getting them. Maybe join a bike gang. "Why would we want to look like Hell's Angels"? He would say. That's how he put it. There was no reasoning with the man, so I stopped discussing anything with him.

They told me I would be a while, to eat something. Keep your electrolytes up. I decided to get something to do with my sport. I designed it myself with the help of Jeremy's tattoo artist, and I knew where I wanted it. Jeremy came with me. There was no pain, just a slight uncomfortable prick repeatedly. Two hours later, the tattoo was finished. Fabulous! I was so excited. We headed home to make lunch, and I called my youngest from the kitchen. As we were talking about my experience, convincing one of the kids from the biker gang to get a tattoo as well, I started losing my balance. Before I knew it, I was kissing the ceramic tile. Elizabeth heard me go down from the phone. She waited and heard nothing from my end. I must have thrown the cell when I landed nose-first on the kitchen floor. I woke to a puddle of blood and a considerable face ache. I had broken my nose. This would be the third time now. My face now suited the biker gang look. As a coincidence, or maybe not, my youngest is now a tattoo artist. That didn't go over well with the ex, but now, years later, he has a tattoo. There's still hope.

Women's' Intuition

I picked up my youngest from high school for a lunch date. As we pulled into the Wendy's restaurant parking lot, a dirty looking character in a white van pulled in beside us. My daughter and I both were like, "Yuck, what a creep." We ordered food and sat down to eat. A few minutes later, the creep pulled out right in front of the restaurant window and stared us down. It was time for us to leave, but I had no keys. I must have left them at the order counter. When I went up, the clerk said she saw them, but they were gone. We asked everyone in the restaurant, but they were now MIA. Elizabeth and I looked at each other and together said, "That creep has got them." I don't know why … intuition, but our gut instinct was to find him. We phoned my dad to pick up another set from my place and take Elizabeth back to school. As we were doing this, Elizabeth spotted the creep in his running van watching us from across the street. She ran towards his van, taking pictures with her phone. He took off like a shot.

We had to call the cops. Something strange was going on. The police were rude as if we were wasting his time. We are keeping him from his donut shop. He did nothing to follow up on our hunch because that's all it was. I drove an old Beamer, that creep must have thought we lived in a mansion. My house keys on that ring. This guy was a criminal, and we needed to find those keys.

My dad took her back to school, and I went back to work. The next day, I called the church, where I rented the gym for my evening fitness classes. I told the church secretary my story, as the master key to the church was on the missing keyring. She'd have to call the key cutters to produce another key by tomorrow. Later that day, the church's secretary called me to tell me she was in possession of my keys.

That morning, one of our sweet, power walking seniors in the neighborhood was out for his walk. He found them a mile away from the restaurant in a park. He was smart enough to see the company's security key and returned them. All those keys are registered. This one was registered to my church. My Angels never sleep.

That creep took my keys, but when he saw Elizabeth taking his picture, he fled to the lake. He must have thrown my keys out the window into the park. Another case solved. I called the officer back to let him know that my daughter and I were right about our hunch. This shit happens all the time. Always go with your gut instinct.

Graduation, Leo Strikes Again

Two years later, at Elizabeth's Grade Twelve graduation, we were all standing for pictures. Leo was there with his girlfriend, soon to be wife. I liked her. She was a pleasant diversion with no baggage. I'd left my shoes at the door, and she'd slipped right into them. Perfect. That didn't take long. I knew that I would never get married again!

We were all standing outside in a garden atrium. Parents were busy with grad photos making their dinner arrangements. My older daughters were quietly calling the restaurant to move the dinner reservations, as we were running late. But silly me, what was I thinking? I wasn't invited. Why would the mother of her child be invited to a family celebration? This would have been an excellent time for Leo to find courage and have us all at the same dinner. I was friends with his girlfriend, and we had no issues with each other. But no, my daughters were caught in the middle of Leo's bullshit again, as he tried to hurt me through them. They all walked away and left me standing there. His girlfriend turned and said, "Sorry, Emily." Elizabeth grabbed me and hugged me so hard. She had tears in her eyes. This was her special day, and he killed it.

She said, "Mom, I don't want to go with them. I want to be with you." I said, "No, go be with the family. I will be ok." I love you baby girl."

Leo loved it. Taking his knife and turning it slowly, watching me squirm.. But I didn't, I was getting stronger. If Leo only knew his hatred for me was hurting his relationships with his daughters. This time the brick he was laying on my shoulder missed. One day when that wall tumbles down, he will be under it. I believe karma does come back to bite you in the butt.

This might not be the end of his games, but I'm not playing anymore. Take your damn ball and go home.

My friend, Patricia, was watching the entire scene. She grabbed my arm and asked me to join her family. Small blessings. He put our family into plenty of those situations. I chose to rise above and be the bigger person. It reminded me of why I'd left him.

33

CHAPTER THIRTY-THREE:

Fifty in Paris

*M*y sister Lesley had the best idea for my fiftieth—a trip to Europe. We never got to spend a considerable amount of time together after she moved out west. She lived an hour away now, but our schedules were crazy. This would be a discovery for both of us. We both had a lot on our plates, but this time was for us. It was also an eye-opener for both of us.

Lesley wanted to celebrate my fiftieth birthday in one of our favorite places. She laid out an itinerary for us before we left. Lesley is an organized planner, and I'm the wingman. She purchased a copy of Rick Steeves's travel guidebook, and away we went. We were on fire. Lesley and Rick took us through Paris in five days flat.

This was the first time since she'd left at sixteen that we spent more than a few days alone together. I don't think she realized we both shared an appreciation for art and ancient architecture. I was on an emotional roller coaster at the time dealing with psycho-Jeremy in my driveway. I wasn't sure if I would find him dead when I returned home. She felt I wasn't enjoying myself and should be living more in the moment with her, but I was in the moment with her, and I loved the time together.

We stayed at an Airbnb in the 7th *Arrondissement.* Our place was around the corner from the Notre Dame Cathedral and walking distance to William Shakespeare's bookstore, the Seine River, and more. We put on the miles, like most tourists. We had the ice cream, sat in the local cafes for fresh croissants, placed a lock on the lock bridge, and picnicked in the park.

It was the end of another day when we walked by Notre Dame Cathedral. We were sitting on the steps, waiting to meet my nephew and his wife who'd just arrived from Ireland. French police were taping off the Notre Dame entry, and news reporters were preparing for their newscasts.

We were in the middle of something. My sister, always loving the action, asked a reporter what was going on. The reporter shared information privy to no one: "Today same-sex marriage became legal in France, and a French far-right historian committed suicide at the altar of the church." Big wow. History in the making at one of the oldest churches in Paris.

Time for a drink. After an exhausting day, we found ourselves at a restaurant across from Notre Dame. We were enjoying people watching and just soaking up the ambiance. While discussing the new layout of the *Musée* d'Orsay, my sister asked me if I liked my wine. "It's okay," I replied.

She blurted out to our waiter, "Excuse me, sir. This wine is shit!"

"Excusez-Moi?" he replied.

She repeated, "This wine is shit. How dare you serve this crappy wine to tourists? I paid good money for that. Bring us a good glass of wine!"

I stared at my sister, kicked her from under the table, and said, "Lesley, you can't talk to him like that."

She replied, "I can say whatever the fuck I want." I'd never seen my sister like this before. Her husband said she was feisty, and he was right. She then looked at me and blurted out, "I don't even know you. Who are you?"

Goodness, I thought. *I'm your sister for shit's sake.* In all honesty, though, we missed twenty-one years of each other's lives, except for random visits.

I replied, "You don't know me? How can I tell you who I am and what I have become when I don't even know who I am?" Bloody hell, I was a mess.

That shitty glass of wine opened the door for one of the best heartfelt conversations we'd ever had. We needed that trip, that explosive conversation. Thank you, Paris.

34

CHAPTER THIRTY-FOUR:

My Crack House

*H*ow can I say no to a young woman and her aunt? They seemed sincere. Now I know, always get references and police checks before renting your home. They were good tenants at first, steady with the rent until a few months went by, and I didn't hear from them. The Aunt dropped off the face of the earth. Things changed, and I could not get a hold of her. I had a hard time collecting the rent. She was never home during the day, but what I didn't know was that she was up to no good during the night. She and a girlfriend ran a little pay for sex operation to purchase heroin—in my sweet retired little neighborhood.

One day I received a tip from a friend at a local printing business. "Emily, I had a strung-out girl come into our print shop looking to make some adjustments on a lease you have with her."

"Holy shit, I've been trying to track that girl down for months," I replied. "Thank you so much for notifying me. I'm driving back into town tomorrow."

She'd used white-out over the name, dates, and amount we'd agreed on. The agreement was now null and void. It was time to call the authorities and have her physically removed.

The next day I met with a police officer in front of my home. He already had Ashley in the back seat. She was screaming on the street. The window was unrolled, and I didn't recognize her. She looked like Brittany Spears when she had her break-down. Ashley had shaved her head and eyebrows. She'd dropped thirty pounds and was wearing a wig, sideways. The ponytail was coming out of her cheek. She couldn't afford rent, but she had enough for heroin and a Pekingese dog. Priorities!

The cops were looking for her boyfriend, as he'd jumped his parole. Her so-called Aunt was her Mother-in-law. I guess more than one person was looking for a tenant. There have been a few cases of break-ins on my quaint little street this past summer. I'm guessing it was Ashley and her burnout pimp and his friends. The officer allowed me to enter my house while she stayed in the cop car. It was in a state.

There were mattresses in every room, with pinholes on all the entries of each wall with sheets for curtains. Burn holes dotted the hardwood floors, counters, and sinks. One bedroom had a padlock on the door. Broken furniture, condom wrappers, and beer bottle caps filled the closets. All my windows had to be replaced.

Lovely. My home was turned into the red-light district of Amsterdam. She had a ceramic mushroom in my front garden. When the light was on, she was open for business.

I walked out furious. Was I in a nighttime police drama? Where are the cameras?

I approached the cop car, staring at that ridiculous wig and white velour tracksuit with no underwear? She was a beauty. I said, "Ashley, I'd stay in the back of that cruiser for your good because if I get my hands on you, I don't know what I'll do."

The police officer said he couldn't hold her on anything and would have to let her go. She wanted to speak to me. The officer unrolled the window of the cruiser, and she said in her best crack-addict, sleepy stuttering voice, "E-e-e-Emily, y-y-y-your h-h-h-h-h-house is hh-hard to t-t-t-take care of!"

Well, of course, it is, you idiot, when you're higher than a kite or lying on the floor getting fucked all the time. How can you possibly get anything done!

The officer opened the back door of the cruiser, and she stumbled out of the car. We both watched her do the walk of shame down my street, with her dog in one hand, and the other holding up her pants until she was out of sight. I looked at the cop and cracked up. I couldn't stop laughing. "Holy shit, did that just happen?" I said

My neighbors later informed me that her pimp wanted his money, my house was broken into, and my neighbors' vehicles were vandalized. I had no idea. My friends proceeded to tell me crazy stories about wallets missing, cars broken into, and chasing this pimp down towards the lake. Wow, a real crime-show in my home and on my street.

I apologized to all my neighbors. This is going to take more than an apple pie to fix. I immediately moved back in to restore the red-light district to the way it was before I left. I learned that the signal for men was a solar ceramic mushroom sitting in my front garden. That was an expensive lesson. Get proper references and a police check. I'll never rent to a heroin attack again.

35

CHAPTER THIRTY-FIVE:

The lake was waiting for me

*O*ne Saturday afternoon, I was visiting Jeremy and the pups. I always went there on weekends to walk the dogs. They spent five days inside, and I gave them the weekends to run. Jeremy was talking about leaving town for good. He was stressed and depressed. He started hating everything around him but his garden.

As I mentioned earlier, my grandfather bought property up north after the Second World War and divided it up amongst his children. Our family spent our summers there. Jeremy's grandparents had property somewhere up north too, and he thought it would do him some good to get in touch with nature. I took him up to my parents' cottage on the sweetest spring-fed lake around. This place was home to me. I loved coming up as a kid and then with the family. I never wanted to leave.

We went up in November. We were out with the dogs for a long walk, following a road that led us towards the water. He said, "Holy shit, this is my grandparents' cottage! They sold that property years ago." Now that's a coincidence. Or was it? There are over 300,000 little lakes in the area.

The following spring, Jeremy and I went up again to clear the roads of broken trees. We noticed a small cottage up for sale. I wanted to book a viewing to see the property. I knew the owners, which might help in the deal. It was a fixer-upper, but it had good bones. Jeremy was handy, and he needed to keep his mind busy. Perfect. He could live there for free and do my Renos until he found a job and eventually moved somewhere else.

I went back home, posted my house on Kijiji, and shebang, it sold in a few days. I then bought the place on the lake, four hours north of the city: fresh air, trees, and a spring-fed lake. We loaded up a considerable U-Haul and away we went. The deal was that he could live rent-free and help me with my Renos. He could then build his tiny home in my driveway and move further north when he found his piece of land.

The Nightmare Unravels

We arrived with the Uhaul and unloaded all the contents of the lake-house onto the lawn. We unloaded our things and put them in the Bunkie next to the house. We began tearing the insides apart, flooring, kitchen, everything. It was a big job, but the weather was cooperating, and Jeremy was working for me. By the end of the summer we moved in, it was sweet. I was so happy to be living on my lake, and I notice a considerable improvement in Jeremy's mental health. We were both happy. Our age difference (he was much younger) hung over our heads, even though it was a platonic relationship, but we both loved each other. Our souls needed to be together for some reason.

My next-door neighbor was going to a personal trainer in town. She introduced me to Miriam, and we became immediate friends and work partners. I started teaching fitness classes at her fitness studio. Jeremy found work as well.

We worked on the place together. I felt like I was at home, finally. I had my dogs on my little piece of heaven. I was in my happy place, where I thought I always belonged, but Jeremy was unsettled again. He was sick of his co-workers; he kept saying they were all stupid and that he hated people. It was time for another project. He was building a tiny home for himself in our driveway, and it was coming along fine. He was short on money to finish it and getting very stressed and blaming everyone around him for his failures. He started to hurt himself and get angry at absolutely nothing.

I tried helping him out by buying books for him to read and finding TED talks to watch about depression. One time we drove to the community hospital and waited a couple of hours in Emergency. Jeremy was in and out in ten minutes. This man was suicidal; he had cuts on his arms, and they wrote him a script for an antidepressant. I was furious. Wow, they didn't even send him for physiological analysis. The drugs, combined with other substances, were making him sick. What's happened to our health care system? It was hard to put any value in our mental health system. This man required help; he wanted it, and they failed him.

I found a therapist for him to see, but he was an hour away. Jeremy agreed to go. That visit lasted five minutes. Jeremy was on the defensive and felt it was two against one. He stomped out and was going to leave me in this small town an hour from home. I ran out after him, jumped in the back of the truck, and screamed, "Stop this truck! Don't leave me here, for fuck's sake."

He stopped and yelled, "Get in the fucking truck, Emily, and do not open your mouth the entire ride home, or I will hurt both of us."

I finally realized I couldn't help this person. He was on the edge and dangerous. I had to sit tight, get home, and lock the doors. He was in his tiny home by then and was living in my driveway.

A few nights later, I called and told him that I was going to be late and asked him to go into the house and check on the puppies.

He replied, "I can't do that for you. I'm not in the mood for fuck sakes," I'd had enough. My husky had puppies and needed someone to check on them.

I said, "You have to; there are three newborn pups in a box in that house with the mother, and I need you to go check. Please!"

"I will, but I'm in no mood to go into your perfect house. I hate you and all your shit."

He was in one of his evil moods. We lived in the middle of nowhere, in the woods, and he was my only hope to look in on the puppies.

When I got home, he was on the living room floor playing with the puppies. I thought, *great, the dogs are okay. Maybe the puppies changed his mood.* He rose from the floor and looked at me. His eyes were two large pools of black, staring me down.

"Thanks," I said. "Did you have dinner yet?" I'm not sure what happened after that. We started arguing, and he started talking crazy. He was ranting that he hated everything about me, about the house, and that he couldn't stand my clutter and the stuff I bought. He was having a shit fit. At that point, he pulled out his small knife. When he got upset, he would cut himself. I didn't want any part of that, and I didn't want to witness it, so I told him to get out.

At the same time, I thought it was a good idea to put some space between us. The arguing got worse, so I opened the door to push him outside. Before I knew it, my hands were on his chest and around his neck. It was the first time I was afraid of him. His back hit the railing, and he was off-balance. He started kicking things, and I ran back inside and locked the door. I thought he was going to go into his home and sleep it off, but then I heard his truck take off.

That's when I knew he had cracked. He needed space from me and me from him. I needed to get the police involved for my protection. I put cameras upon the property. He was removed in the spring when the ice started to melt. Then I had a major clean up. That night shook me up. I found out later on that Jeremy moved back south.

So what was that all about? I spent years trying to help someone who didn't want to help himself. Was I punishing myself for the pain I caused Leo and my family? Why else would I have done this to myself? Am I not worthy of love? I also know now, people who say," I'm going to kill myself," don't kill themselves, its just a big cry for help. Jeremy once told me, he would cut himself, inflict pain on himself, because he wants to feel that instead of the voices in their head.

36

CHAPTER THIRTY-SIX:
The Reading

I went home for a short visit. I needed to gather my thoughts. Surround myself with people I loved. I needed to feel loved. My closet girlfriend set up a night for a medium to come to the house. This person entered her house downstairs, and there was no eye contact with anyone. He did not know who he was reading or what spirits would arrive. He called on us by the dead who came to see one of us. It was my turn as he shouted up the stairs, who's Jeremy?

As I proceeded to go downstairs, my palms were sweating, and my heart was racing from excitement. I needed some answers. There was an open sofa, and I sat across from the medium knee to knee.

He began to talk about my Chi, my energy around me. He began to tell me, my journey with Jeremy is over. He's not my patient nor my lover. I do not owe him anything, and he has nothing to give in this life to anyone.

He said, "I was supposed to die at sixteen, but it wasn't my time." I remember a car accident, but we walked from it. At that age, you felt as if you were infallible. Guaranteed nothing will ever happen to you, and if it did, you didn't ponder on the outcome. Frontal lobe thinking. The rational part of the brain is not connected, so kids do stupid stuff.

I asked the medium, "Why is your left ear so red"? He replied, "The spirits were talking all at once." They were using him as a channel to talk to me. I was in awe. They all came to see me. To tell me something.

First was my cousin John, my cousin that had recently passed to the lake. He told me to keep smiling, and to keep wearing that dress, the one with the red flower on it, you sparkle when you are in it". He also said, "tell Uncle Desi, my father, that the Maple Leafs will make the playoffs.

Now I am dreaming, lol.

There was a little boy, a spirit, jumping on the sofa, he wanted to tell me he was my brother, my younger brother that died before his birth. His name was Desi. He is with me always. There were more words said, then my time was up. I felt at peace.

Our family never spoke of that time. It was a sad time for my parents. But I needed to know.

Lesley was in town visiting. We took our mother out for lunch. During the meal, I brought up my reading, and the visitors I had from heaven. I told her about the little boy. I said, "Mom, there was a little boy. He was small and wiry. He said he was my brother." "Were you going to name that baby boy Desi?" "Yes, after your father," she replied. "Well, Desi Jr. is fine and happy and stays with me always." There was silence. That's a lot to swallow. Hard to believe for most.

I drove back up north the next day ready to start down a new path, but when I pulled into my driveway, seeing Jeremy's tiny house, the emotions came flooding back.

37

THIRTY-SEVEN:

My Epiphany

*I*t was on January six. The starting of a new year fo myself. I was exhausted. I'd been through a lot, so I slept for a couple of days. I couldn't believe it was over. I was safe. I started asking myself, *how do I get myself into these relationships? What's my next move?* That night I stepped outside I needed some fresh air. It was -30 out. It was clear, and the night sky was deep. I'm a massive star gazing geek, and there is no light pollution where I live. I and headed down to my dock. It was covered in snow as I lay down to rest. The tears started to run, filling my ears. It was time to ask the universe, *What now? Why did I come to the lake? Now that you got me up here, what do you want with me?* I'd been through enough.

Just then, the most glorious, shooting star I have ever seen zoomed past my lake, right over my head, and headed west. It was so beautiful, and the timing was impeccable. *Was that a sign?*

I lay there for a while, basking in the afterglow of the star. I went back inside, but that memory on my calendar, washed my face and went to bed. I slept better than I had in years and woke feeling so much lighter. I needed my life back. It was a new day, a fresh start. I was officially done with men and helping people for a while. Now the clean-up could begin. It was time to light a fire and get to work.

Fun fact: January Six is the Epiphany. The feast of the Three Kings. They celebrate it twelve days after Christmas. This day honors the revelation of God incarnate as Jesus Christ. For me, it was my death and beginning of a new life — an original painting.

Jeremy was a collector of junk. My place looked like it was off the television show, Sanford and Sons. I called the Got-Junk guy, and he removed as much as he could from my property. What was I going to do with all the tires? Why did he have so many? What is it with men? I wish you could remove people that way. Just call the "My man is fucked truck." Just pick him up and throw him in. I could give this guy a steady business. Can I collect Air Miles?

I remember one night the power went out, and my sump pumps stopped. I needed to get them working. To avoid flooding, I pulled on my rubber boots and headed to my walkout basement. It was blacker than the ace of spades out, and the bitter cold made my nostrils stick together when I inhaled. Canadian winters in the north are bitterly cold. I was down below in the dark pumping water when I heard my chickens squawking. I ran to the chicken coop to find Cinnamon cornered by a fox. We had given our chickens stripper names.

I released my dogs on the fox. Good boys. My cousin performed a little reiki on Cinnamon, and she was as good as new. Later that winter, my beautiful blue-eyed husky pup slaughtered all my free-range chickens but one. Cinnamon was the only survivor of the massacre. I froze all my fine feathered ladies and fed them to my husky. There was a lesson in it for me. My girlfriends and parents told me to come home. They said I'd been through enough. I told them I was home, that I needed to be there. My peace would now return without Jeremy around.

As I said before, I never go backward. Never. This is my life, and I am supposed to be here. Through all this, my mother wanted me to find a nice man and settle down. Someone to take care of my needs. After what I've been through? I told her I was never getting married again, that I don't need a man. I also knew in my heart that I wouldn't be alone, that my prince was somewhere. I just wasn't ready for him yet.

I didn't want a born and bred northern man. They're a different breed altogether. I knew I wasn't settling down up here forever, but the lake was a great home base when I was traveling.

There was a reason for my presence on this lake in the middle of nowhere. Through all the craziness, there was an underlying peace. The lake has been my constant since I can remember.

It is my home.

Car Fire

Nothing is simple for me. I removed all the junk from my property, as well as the man. Now I had a car to sell, but I lived in the middle of nowhere. I parked my car at a local country store parking lot and put a for sale sign on it. There was more traffic on the regional road than my cottage road. One afternoon, I received a phone call from an angry parent. He wanted to know if I was the owner of the car his son was test driving. I didn't realize someone was testing the vehicle today. He said there was a problem with the vehicle. His son got half a mile from the store, and it started smoking. He pulled into a drive of a horse farm, where the car burst into flames. I apologized, and the man said his son was fine. Thank goodness nobody was hurt.

I arrived later at the farmer's house to see the pile of metal that was once my car. The only thing that had color remaining was my door handle. What is it with me and cars? The universe was y telling me something. I needed to start taking the bus.

But first, I needed to call Got Junk again to pick up this pile of burnt metal.

38

CHAPTER-EIGHT:
Sammy Fowers

J was settling in nicely with my new life. It was time for me to start painting my picture, living my life through my eyes only, and doing things my way, answering to no one. Asking no one. I hear old blue eyes, Frank Sinatra sing, "I did it my way."

It was Valentine's Day, and I was at the fitness studio where I worked. I was just about to go into class when a beautiful bouquet arrived for me. It was signed, "Your Secret Admirer."

Miranda, the owner of the studio, said, "that's romantic." I asked, "Is that cool or creepy?".

In my headspace, it was creepy. For anyone else, it would have been romantic. We are in the middle of Whoville. I want to be left alone. I didn't give it much thought and continued teaching classes and cleaning homes. A week or so later, another arrangement arrived at the studio with the same card. *Wow, what's with this guy? Are men that sweet?* I thought chivalry was dead.

I received a phone call at the weekend. It was from the guy who sent the flowers. I asked him why he sent the flowers and how we knew each other. "I was sitting at a stoplight, and a voice told me to look up, and I did," he said. "I saw you. You were crossing the road from the bank to the building. At the time, I had no clue who you were, but I just knew I had to meet you. I just knew you were going to be in my life, and I wasn't sure in what capacity." Before the light turned green, I looked up at the building and saw a business advertisement with a picture of you and your co-worker on it. So, I knew you worked in the building. It was Valentine's Day, and I thought to myself, it's been a while since I sent flowers to a woman, so I called the florist and had them deliver a bouquet to you."

He sounded nice. I told him I'd been through a lot and wasn't interested in anything right now. He was polite and said he respected that. I thought about it some more and felt I should at least meet the guy for coffee. He didn't sound like a hillbilly or psycho killer. A few days later, I called him back, and we met for coffee. He wasn't a typical northern boy, attached to his snowmobiles and hunting guns, without a dental plan. Sam was from the south, like me. He was a city boy; he grew up an hour away from my hometown. I thought I should at least buy him a coffee or lunch to thank him for the flowers.

I was sitting at a table at Twigs Coffee Shop when Sam walked in. He looked tired and his ski- jacket looked way too big for him. Why did I feel sorry for him?

Stop analyzing people, I thought. *He doesn't need help, Emily.* He just looked like a lost dog in a snowstorm. He said he'd moved up north nine years ago with his wife to live in the woods and get away from the city. I told him I moved up three years ago, but I'd been coming up to my parents' lake since I was born. Oddly enough, Sam had been coming up for years to go fishing with his buddies. He lived ten minutes from me, just down the highway.

Sam's wife had recently passed away from a long battle with cancer. That explained the sullen look. We talked for a while. There was an easy way about him. He was very chill and easy to talk too. It felt as if we'd met before. We finished our drinks and said goodbye. Before I left, I asked him, "Do you have a wood-burning fireplace? Where do you get your wood from?"

He gave me the guy's name, and I called him. I was so excited to get a wood delivery. Jeremy had cleaned me out of all my tools, including the chainsaw and wood splitter, so I had to rent what I needed.

Soon a massive truck towing enough wood to build a small log cabin arrived on my property. I asked the driver, "Are those trees all for me?"

He took one look at my place and laughed. "Are you heating that place with this wood? You got yourself enough for four winters."

"Great," I said. "Now, where do I start?"

I know what you're thinking: call the lonely guy in the woods to help. I did.

"Hey Sam, it's Emily. I've got a load of wood that requires cutting, splitting, and piling. Do you know where I can rent a chainsaw and splitter?"

He laughed. "No worries, I'll do it for you. I have all the equipment here." I was hoping he would say that.

He showed up Saturday morning with bells on.

"I always wondered what was at the end of this road," he said. "I've driven by it for the last thirty years."

"I am," I said. I jumped into the action, trying to help. I had to throw the cut wood for splitting, but I have a bum hand, so I was pretty much useless. He just took over. He was a man on a mission. He worked like the Energizer Bunny. He stopped for a sip of water and was right back at it. I figured he had stuff on his mind or some pent-up energy he had to release.

He returned a few days later to work again. I had to get to work, so we made some small talk and away I went. I told my friends at the building that Sammy Flowers (his nickname) was a great guy and a widower. I should introduce him to one of our single clients. Maybe one of the ladies would like to meet him.

"Maybe he likes you," Miranda said.

"Good luck with that. I gave men up for Lent for the next decade. Besides, neither of us are looking for anything right now."

The next day he showed up with his homemade applesauce. Homemade applesauce? Really? The man makes his own sauce. Who was this guy? Paul Bunyan, and he cooks? But wait the topper, he makes lip-chap. This is a man that takes care of his lips. Now that's a person I can get to know?

After he was finished, he asked me out for a drink or dinner. I honestly didn't want to have a drink with him, but dinner would be nice.

We had a great time. There was a calmness about him. He was funny and had so many exciting stories about people he'd met bartending. But it was his smile that got me. I know that smile.

We talked about our childhoods, high school, and our past work experiences. It seemed like Sam, and his wife stayed reclusive after she took ill. They never had kids of their own, so there was no baggage, and I wasn't about to throw all my luggage on the table. Nobody wants that. We took a walk on the waterfront before heading back to his truck. I leaned over and asked for a kiss.

He was a fabulous kisser. They were so soft. It must be lip-chap. I thought I had kissed those lips before, but when, and where? It had been a long time since I had a kiss that took my breath away.

Before I knew it, my mind was teleported back to Paris, Back to the *Moulin Rouge*. I was Nicole Kidman, and Sam was Ewan McGregor. We were standing face to face starring into each others' eyes. The music cued. Sam opened his mouth, and Ewan's voice spewed out,

Never knew I could feel like this,
Like I've never seen the sky before.
I want to vanish inside your kiss,
Every day I'm loving you more and more.
Listen to my heart, can you hear it sings,
Telling me to give you everything.
Seasons may change, winter to spring,
But I love you until the end of time....
Now we reach the high notes and sing together,

Come what may, I will love you until my dying day.

I thought to myself, and *I will keep that little brain fart to myself.*

Our next date was at his place. Sam offered to cook dinner for me. Now, you must remember that I hadn't had a man cook me a meal in over thirty years ... not that I can remember. The only time I ever dated, the man had to be able to cook. Maybe it was a test, in general, to build up some credibility, I don't know. Perhaps I just wanted somebody to cook me a meal, maybe fold my laundry.

I found myself on my way to Sam's. It was funny, and I knew his neck of the woods. Years ago, when I was training, I would cycle past his place.

Dinner was delicious again. I found myself so comfortable with this person, and it was easy to talk to him. We made each other laugh. I noticed he was very intuitive as well. Once he got serious and asked me if I was okay. Was I in any danger? Then he told me about a dream he'd had. He'd seen me pushing a man out of my back door with my hands on his neck. It was a confrontation of some sort, and then the man ran off. My heart was beating a mile a minute, and my palms were sweating. I said I wasn't in danger anymore, but I was put in that situation a few months ago.

I found myself spending more time with Sammy on the lake and over at his place. We had a great connection. I was still standing my ground with a wall around me, still hating men, but Sam was slowly taking down that wall, brick by brick. I went to his place for another meal and told him about that night when I was so sad and feeling desperate and lay down on the snowy dock in the cold, asking the universe for help. It was January 6. I remembered it so vividly.

"There was a magnificent shooting star that traveled west, towards your place. I will never forget that moment."

He just sat there, and his jaw dropped. "I remember that night. It was cold, and the night was clear. I was out in the backyard, with the dog, looking up at the sky and feeling lost, the way you were. The air was heavy with despair. Then that same shooting star crossed my path. It was spectacular. I remember it well. Maybe it was a sign; maybe it was for us."

"Whatever it was, it saved my life," I said. "The next day, when I woke up, I had no reason to be sad. I saw a new beginning."

I drove home that night feeling so much better. I was thinking about how fast life changes, how one minute you're feeling so down and out, and in the next breath, you feel complete. Sam and I spent more and more time together. We enjoyed each other's company. I felt like we were picking up where we left off.

One night over dinner (he cooked, of course) we started to discuss where we grew up, what our high schools were like, and what we did as kids. We must have crossed paths at a track meet. He lived an hour away, but in those days, without social media, like Facebook or Instagram, Sam could have lived ten hours away.

I told him I spent my weekends hanging out with my girlfriends and related a few stories about driving over the river to Niagara Falls, New York. It made him laugh. I told him my father's family was from Niagara Falls, and that I loved walking the gorge and enjoying the sights. He said he used to go there too. He said he enjoyed it down there as a kid, and he used to head over the river with a buddy of his. They would drink themselves silly at bars and then drive home.

We realized that we had more in common than we thought because as young teenagers, we did a lot of the same things. We were both fun-loving spirits who loved to make people laugh. We were both athletic and competitive in track and field and other sports. We also talked about the bars that we both visited over the bridge to the States. Then he got a funny look on his face. "Have you ever been to Club Exit?" he asked.

I explained that I'd been there a few times with a girlfriend and that I'd met a lot of guys over there. I told him that we'd head from there to the Flying Saucer for Saucer Fries and then drive back home. It was always a good night.

Then we looked at each other.

"Were you at Club Exit one night, maybe with your sister? I was with my friend Buster, a tall blonde kid. We were at the bar, and we had just grabbed drinks."

I told him I'd never been over the river drinking with my sister, but when we met guys from out of town, my girlfriend and I always said that we were sisters, to get a rise out of the guys we met. I looked at him. We were thirty-six years older, and it's hard to remember everyone you've met in your past, but I looked deep into his eyes, and I saw that smiley, devilish seventeen-year-old boy, the one I met that night.

"You were the one with the mischievous smile!"

We were both so taken back.

"Was that you that night? You and your (sister) girlfriend took us to the Flying Saucer after we partied all night."

"Yes!" I replied. "That was me!" I think I was blushing, and he certainly was. We couldn't stop smiling. "Oh, my God! I wondered what happened to you, but you didn't give me your phone number", I said. "No, I didn't," he replied.

"I think I have something of yours. Hold on," said Sam. He came back with a watch. It was a Mickey Mouse watch with a red band and cracked crystal.

"Where did you get this?"

"I don't know," he said. "I've had it for years, but I think it's yours."

Another jaw-dropping moment.

"OMG It is mine," I said. I hadn't seen it in over forty years. It had a lady's band on it, and it was worn out at a particular hole. It fit me perfectly. My boomerang won't come back, but my watch did!

I was Cinderella, and he was my prince with the glass slipper.

Samuel's Reading

Sam wanted to connect with his deceased wife. He was told of a channeler a few hours away. It was suggested by a friend to see this person. He called her, and she said it wasn't his wife's time, that she was too weak to cross over. She'd let him know when he could speak with her.

He received a call and was told to come on her birthday. He was astounded, to say the least. So off he went. Sam drove south and showed up for the reading. The first thing out of the woman's mouth was, "Hey, where's my birthday cake?"

"Pardon me?" said Sam.

"It's my birthday, so where's my cake?"

They spoke for over an hour through this medium.

"So how do you like Emily?" she asked.

Again, Sam's mouth dropped. He replied, "How do you about Emily?"

"She's one of us, Sam. Emily has traveled centuries with all of our souls. We saw that you were both so sad and desperate, we thought it was a good time to put you both back together."

That's what I meant when I said, "My universe answered my prayers!"

39

CHAPTER THIRTY-NINE:

The Proper Proposal

*I*t was October 9, Sam's birthday, when the moon was so full, it cast its reflection on the water. We were out on the lake, stargazing in the red canoe. We enjoyed the northern night skies together. It was a summer of getting to know each other and making up for lost time. We stopped paddling and were floating, enjoying the moment. Sam got up, held onto the gunnels of the canoe, and walked towards me. I said, "Stop, you're going to tip us! I'll kiss you when we get to shore, silly." He proceeded to get down on one knee.

Sam pulled a ring from his jeans pocket. He said after that he'd been carrying it for months, right after he asked my father for my hand in marriage.

I was stunned. Who does this? Am I in a Hallmark movie? I thought to myself, *Do I want this, especially after I said, "I will never marry again, never allow a man to hurt me." But this is the man from my dreams, the man standing over me, removing the bricks from my body, as my body laid there still as can be, he offered a hand to me, now I must take it.*

I didn't know what to say, but I didn't have to think of an answer. It just came out: "Yes! Yes, I will marry you."

It was so perfect—the setting, the romantic proposal. Everything I ever wanted was in this person. I guess the universe wasn't ready to put Sam and me together at seventeen. I believe now I had to have my girls, experience my journey with Leo. Grow from that experience and have another. I also think it was my relationship with Jeremy that brought me up north and back to my home in the woods and Sam. I think we both had work to do before the universe put our souls back together. We had a beautiful barn wedding with all our family and friends. It was a magical day that I'd never forget. In the eyes of everyone there, we were two adult people, in love with each other and life, but for Sam and me, we were those two kids from long ago, starting our lives together.

I can see clearly now

It still brings tears to my eyes how blessed I am to have such a lovely man in my life. I wrote this book as a healing tool for myself, like a journal. As I started on this journey, I had some anger, and some hostility still burning in me. It lingered. But as I started writing, it was all was diffused. I learned a lot about myself and my acceptance of others why they are in my life, my fears, my tears and most of all, my journey. Never say never, and always follow your heart. Trust that little voice inside of you. Your intuition and your faith. I have arrived!

I am now awakened, transformed by my suffering. I would not change an event that happened, just my reactions to those events.

This poem took me through my worst times to my best times. William Earnest Henley wrote this poem, "Invictus." It's one of my favorite poems and gave me the strength to push on.

Invictus

Out of the night that covers me,
Black as the pit from pole to pole,
I thank whatever gods maybe
For my unconquerable soul.

In the fell clutch of circumstance
I have not winced nor cried aloud.
Under the bludgeoning's of chance
My head is bloody but unbowed.

Beyond this place of wrath and tears
Looms but the Horror of the shade,
And yet the menace of the years
Finds and shall find me unafraid.

It matters not how strait the gate,
How charged with punishments the scroll,
I am the master of my fate, and I am the captain of my soul.

I love the strength in that poem. It still brings tears to my eyes every time I read it. The first time I read it was in high school. It truly touched me. God gives you a ship for your soul. We're to take that soul on the journey of life. That's why I'm here. That's why we are here. To make mistakes and to learn lessons from them.

I tattooed "Live Your Dash" on my body because I wanted to make that a permanent statement. How I live my life now is through those words. Two dates in your life are milestones: the day you are born and the day you die. The line between is your dash. Think of that dash as your life. You have one life to live. Live it like it's your last. Live it to the fullest. Be kind, and kind people will surround you. Take each waking moment like it's a gift from God. When you wake each morning, be grateful you're there for another day. Live that day like it's the first time you are seeing it. And before you go to bed, thank God for the life you have. That comes from my heart.

Emily P. Zalott
…..and I do!

CPSIA information can be obtained
at www.ICGtesting.com
Printed in the USA
LVHW110414291020
670075LV00022B/404